Student Activity Guide
for

Children
The Early Years

by
Dr. Celia A. Decker, retired
Professor of Family and Consumer Sciences
Northwestern State University of Louisiana
Natchitoches, Louisiana

Publisher
The Goodheart-Willcox Company, Inc.
Tinley Park, Illinois

Introduction

This activity guide accompanies the textbook *Children: The Early Years*. It will help you recall, review, and expand on each chapter you read in the text. It will also help you understand how children grow and develop as well as how to meet their needs.

What's the best way to use this activity guide? First, read your assignment in the text. The activities in the guide complement the chapters in the text. Carefully read the instructions at the beginning of each activity. Then, complete the activity to review what you have learned.

Some of the activities in this guide review the text. You can use them to help you prepare for quizzes and tests. Try to complete as much of the activity as you can without looking up the answers. Once you finish, compare your answers to the information in the book. At this time, complete any questions you could not answer.

Other activities ask for your opinions, evaluations, and conclusions. The answers are your thoughts and cannot be judged as right or wrong. These activities should help you to evaluate situations thoughtfully and to think about alternatives.

Many activities require you to observe children. These will enable you to see firsthand how children look, think, and act. Observation activities give you a chance to work directly with children and find out what they respond to best. Be sure to read these activities carefully and prepare for the observation before you begin. Then, watch children and carefully write down what you observe.

You should find all these activities to be fun and interesting. In addition, what you learn will help you work with children in positive ways now and in the future.

Contents

Part 6: Guiding and Caring for Children

Learning About Children

Parents Aid Children's Growth and Development

Activity A

Chapter 1

Name _____

Date _____ Period _____

Parents are responsible for meeting many needs of their children. For each of the following categories of children's needs, write two specific examples of how parents may meet their children's needs. Share your examples with other members of the class. Then answer the question that follows.

1. Physical needs

    Example A _____

    _____

    Example B _____

    _____

2. Intellectual needs

    Example A _____

    _____

    Example B _____

    _____

3. Social needs

    Example A _____

    _____

    Example B _____

    _____

4. Trust needs

    Example A _____

    _____

    Example B _____

    _____

5. Love/discipline needs

    Example A _____

    _____

    Example B _____

    _____

How do you think studying child development can help parents meet children's needs in better ways?

_____

_____

_____

Individual Life Cycle

Activity B

Chapter 1

Name _____

Date _____ Period _____

Complete the following chart about the individual life cycle.

Stage	Average age (length of time)	Description
Prenatal		
Neonatal		
Infancy		
Toddler		
Preschool		
School-age		

Heredity or Environment?

Activity C

Chapter 1

Name _____

Date _____ Period_____

Both a person's heredity and environment affect growth and development. For the most part, heredity and environment work together. However, genes affect some aspects of development more than others. The same is true for the environment. On the lines below, list some of your traits that you think are mainly products of your heredity. In the next column, list some of your traits that are mainly products of your environment.

Heredity	Environment

Is The Brain More Than a Computer?

Activity D

Chapter 1

Name _____

Date _____ Period_____

People have compared the human brain to many inventions such as the telephone switchboard. Today, the brain is often compared to a computer. For each statement about the computer, write a corresponding statement about the human brain. Share your comparisons with the class.

Computer	Brain
1. Machine (made of metal, plastic, and silicon) that has input devices, a central processing unit, and output devices.	
2. Can be exactly duplicated.	
3. Completely manufactured before it is first used.	
4. Uses electrical signals.	
5. Uses electricity to transmit signals.	
6. Has energy that comes from electricity.	
7. Does not transmit when the power is "off".	
8. Can crash or get sick with a virus or worm.	
9. Can be easily fixed.	
10. Follows a set of instructions to solve problems.	
11. Cannot follow a command it is not programmed to understand. Cannot "learn" from repeated commands.	
12. Does most things one at a time.	
13. Is a fast processor.	
14. Needs to be replaced often with a newer model.	

A Look at Tomorrow

Activity E

Chapter 1

Name _____

Date _____ Period_____

Growth and development are rather constant. Often what children are today gives a hint of what they will be tomorrow. Complete the following descriptions in ways that show constancy of growth and development.

1. **As a young child:** Juan was an active baby who crawled and walked at an early age. As a young child, he liked outside climbing, swinging, and sliding equipment. In play, he showed no fear and performed many movements with skill.

   As an older child: _____

   _____

   _____

   _____

   As a young adult: _____

   _____

   _____

   _____

2. **As a young child:** Rachel's parents are both artists. Rachel was born with "crayons and paintbrushes in her hands." As a toddler, she scribbled on everything, including the walls! When she was enrolled in preschool, her drawings looked more advanced than those of other children. In other areas, she was more like her classmates.

   As an older child: _____

   _____

   _____

   _____

   As a young adult: _____

   _____

   _____

   _____

3. **As a young child:** Justin was a premature baby who always seemed to be getting sick. Out of fear for their son's health, Justin's parents kept him at home and, for the most part, away from other children. His first grade teacher described Justin as "a good student, but very shy."

   As an older child: _____

   _____

   _____

   _____

   As a young adult: _____

   _____

   _____

   _____

(Continued)

Name_____

4. **As a young child:** Marvin was the youngest of six children who were closely spaced. Marvin has always had to share his toys and a bedroom and wait his turn for adult attention. Marvin is a cheerful, easygoing child who adapts easily to other children.

As an older child: _____

_____

_____

_____

As a young adult: _____

_____

_____

_____

5. **As a young child:** Latoya's father is a lawyer and her mother is a chemist. Latoya talked early, and before she entered school, she could read with ease and count her piggy bank savings. Latoya's kindergarten teacher noted she was ahead in all her subjects. Testing during her kindergarten year confirmed that she was very gifted.

As an older child: _____

_____

_____

_____

As a young adult: _____

_____

_____

_____

6. **As a young child:** Kevin's father plays saxophone in a jazz band and his mother sings solos in her church choir. Even as a young baby, Kevin always would tap and "sing" along to the music that was playing in the house. By the age of six, Kevin would hear melodies and play them on the family piano.

As an older child: _____

_____

_____

_____

As a young adult: _____

_____

_____

_____

The Wholeness of Growth and Development

Activity F

Chapter 1

Name _____

Date _____ Period_____

All aspects of growth and development interact with each other. This is true not only for children, but for adults as well. In the following situations, try to imagine how a person might react. Then write how the situations might affect other aspects of that person's development.

Situation #1

Social-emotional aspect: Jane is going on her first date with George next week, and she is excited, but a little nervous about it.

Physical aspect: _____

_____

Mental aspect: _____

_____

Situation #2

Mental aspect: Dwayne's grades have dropped, and he is in danger of failing one or more classes.

Social-emotional aspect: _____

_____

Physical aspect: _____

_____

Situation #3

Social-emotional aspect: Carl overheard friends joking about his weight problem, and he is hurt and embarrassed.

Physical aspect: _____

_____

Mental aspect: _____

_____

Situation #4

Physical aspect: Now that Celia is no longer a child, she has begun to realize that using a wheelchair may cause some problems for her.

Mental aspect: _____

_____

Social-emotional aspect: _____

_____

Children Fulfill Their Needs

Activity G

Chapter 1

Name _____

Date _____ Period _____

Young children strive to fulfill many needs through activities like those listed below. Using chart 1-19 in the text, identify the need being met by each activity below.

Activity	*Need Being Satisfied*
1. drinking water	_____
2. hugging	_____
3. playing with a friend	_____
4. repeating a new word	_____
5. stopping at the street corner before crossing	_____
6. sleeping	_____
7. touching a flower and saying "pretty"	_____
8. showing his or her drawing	_____
9. putting on shoes	_____
10. staying in the yard	_____
11. taking a favorite stuffed toy everywhere	_____
12. smiling and clapping hands after building a block tower	_____
13. eating banana slices	_____
14. visiting a pediatrician	_____
15. moving to music	_____
16. sitting in grandmother's lap	_____
17. holding the stair railing	_____
18. helping "read" a story	_____
19. saying, "Big girl"	_____
20. taking vitamins	_____

Observation: Children at Play

Activity H   Name _____

Chapter 1   Date _____ Period_____

People observe children for many reasons. Observations help you answer questions about children's development and behavior. Observations can give you new ideas about how to work and interact with children. You learn to look for causes that affect their behavior. Observations can help you see how children react to others. For this activity, observe one or more children at play. Record your observation notes on the following page. Then write your responses to the information requested.

1. List the purpose of the observation. _____

   _____

   _____

   _____

2. List the location of observation. _____

   _____

   _____

3. What are the names and ages of children observed? _____

   _____

   _____

   _____

   _____

   _____

4. What new or interesting behaviors did you observe? _____

   _____

   _____

   _____

5. Write your notes and comments about the observation. _____

   _____

   _____

   _____

6. What other information do you need in order to make any conclusions about the observation? _____

   _____

   _____

   _____

7. Time began _____ Time completed _____

(Continued)

Name_____

Observation Notes:

_____
_____
_____
_____
_____
_____
_____
_____
_____
_____
_____
_____
_____
_____
_____
_____
_____
_____
_____
_____
_____
_____
_____
_____
_____
_____
_____
_____
_____
_____
_____

Families Today

Family Types

Activity A

Chapter 2

Name _____

Date _____ Period _____

There are many types of families in America, each type with strengths and weaknesses. Describe the family types listed below and then list some of the strengths and weaknesses of each type.

1. Two-parent family_____

   Strengths _____

   _____

   Weaknesses _____

   _____

2. Single-parent family _____

   Strengths _____

   _____

   Weaknesses _____

   _____

3. Stepfamily_____

   Strengths _____

   _____

   Weaknesses _____

   _____

4. Extended family _____

   Strengths _____

   _____

   Weaknesses _____

   _____

5. Family with adopted children_____

   Strengths _____

   _____

   Weaknesses _____

   _____

6. Foster family_____

   Strengths _____

   _____

   Weaknesses _____

   _____

The Family Life Cycle

Activity B

Chapter 2

Name _____

Date _____ Period _____

The stages of the family life cycle are listed below. Define each stage. Write a short story describing a family and how the family goes through the stages of the life cycle.

Beginning stage: _____

_____

Childbearing stage: _____

_____

Parenting stage: _____

_____

Launching stage: _____

_____

Mid-years stage: _____

_____

Aging stage: _____

_____

Family Life Cycle Story

_____

_____

_____

_____

_____

_____

_____

_____

_____

_____

_____

_____

_____

_____

_____

_____

Types of Discipline

Activity C   Name _____

Chapter 2   Date _____ Period_____

Three types of discipline are listed below. Describe each type. Give an example of how a parent might use this type of discipline. Then give your opinion regarding each type, explaining why it is a good form of discipline or a poor form of discipline. Use your comments as a basis for a class discussion.

Power Assertion: _____

_____

_____

_____

Example: _____

_____

_____

Opinion of technique: _____

_____

_____

Love Withdrawal: _____

_____

_____

_____

Example: _____

_____

_____

Opinion of technique: _____

_____

_____

Induction: _____

_____

_____

_____

Example: _____

_____

_____

Opinion of technique: _____

_____

_____

Parenting Styles

Activity D

Chapter 2

Name _____

Date _____ Period_____

Three parenting styles are listed below. Describe each style. Give an example of how a parent might use this parenting style. Then give your opinion regarding the style, explaining why it is good parenting style or a poor parenting style. Use your comments as a basis for a class discussion.

Authoritarian: _____

_____

_____

Example: _____

_____

_____

Opinion of style: _____

_____

_____

Permissive: _____

_____

_____

_____

Example: _____

_____

_____

Opinion of style: _____

_____

_____

Democratic: _____

_____

_____

_____

Example: _____

_____

_____

Opinion of style: _____

_____

_____

Comparing Parenting to Other Careers

Activity A

Chapter 3

Name _____

Date _____ Period _____

For some parents, parenting is their full-time job. Other parents have careers in addition to parenting. Young adults can prepare for parenthood by comparing parenting to other careers. In the spaces below, use descriptive phrases to show how you think parenting compares to most other careers.

Category	Parenting	Most Other Careers
Preparation received before getting a job		
Job description in terms of how specific or general the responsibility		
Hours of responsibility		
Place of work		
Salary		
Overtime pay		
Pay raises based on merit		

(Continued)

Name_____

Category	Parenting	Most Other Careers
Sick leave policy		
Professional or personal leave policy		
Retirement plan		
Health or life insurance plans		

In terms of responsibilities and training for responsibilities, how does parenting compare with other careers?

_____

_____

_____

_____

In terms of the benefits listed on this chart, how does parenting compare with other careers? _____

_____

_____

_____

List some benefits of parenting that are not included in the chart. _____

_____

_____

_____

How can filling out a chart like this be helpful when deciding whether or not to become a parent?

_____

_____

_____

_____

_____

_____

Child Development Resources

Activity B

Chapter 3

Name _____

Date _____ Period_____

Parents-to-be and parents have many resources available to help them learn child care skills. However, they may not know where to find them. Find some of the resources available in or near your community. You may want to consult your Cooperative Extension Service, American Red Cross Chapter, other local civic or religious organizations, universities or colleges with child development or child care programs, local pediatricians, local libraries or the Internet. List the resources as you locate them.

Professionals in Child Care or Parenting

Name	*Affiliation*

Parenting Classes

Other Resources

Is This a Good Reason for Choosing Parenthood?

Activity C   Name _____

Chapter 3   Date _____ Period_____

The most important reason for wanting children is to share your love with them. Couples who have children for other reasons may be in for some big surprises. With a group of other students in your class, plan a skit about the problems involved in having a child for one of these reasons. Base your skit on one of the themes listed below. Use the space provided to plan your ideas for the skit. Then perform your skit in class.

Skit Theme (check one)

_____   "Wouldn't it be nice to have a cute little baby?"

_____   "Our parents want grandchildren."

_____   "Our older child needs a brother or sister."

_____   "A child can make us proud."

_____   "Others will see me as a stable, reliable person."

_____   "A child will comfort us in our old age."

_____   "A child will make us love each other."

Characters _____

_____

_____

Basic plot of skit _____

_____

_____

_____

_____

_____

_____

_____

_____

_____

_____

_____

_____

_____

_____

_____

_____

_____

Couple Relationships Affect Parenthood

Activity D

Chapter 3

Name _____

Date _____ Period _____

Couples who have strong relationships are more likely to be effective parents than couples whose relationships are weak. Although there is no exact formula to measure a relationship, certain descriptions can show the quality of a relationship. On the lines provided in the left column, list words or phrases that can be used to show a strong relationship. Across from each of these descriptions, list the opposite in the right column. (An example is shown to get you started.) Then answer the question that follows.

Strong Relationships	Weak Relationships
strong trust in boyfriend/girlfriend/spouse	lack of trust

Why do you think it is important for a couple to have a strong relationship in order to be effective parents?

_____

_____

_____

_____

_____

_____

The Cost of Parenthood

Activity E

Chapter 3

Name _____

Date _____ Period _____

Having and caring for children is expensive. Couples need to consider the costs and ways to meet those costs before having children. Interview a couple who has a child or children about the costs of parenthood. Record information from the couple in the space provided.

Name of couple _____

Number and age(s) of child (children) _____

Types of expenses for basic care of child (children) _____

_____

_____

_____

_____

_____

Types of expenses for items not needed, but wanted, for child (children)_____

_____

_____

_____

_____

_____

Types of expenses expected in the future _____

_____

_____

_____

_____

_____

How did having a child (children) change the couple's budget? _____

_____

_____

_____

_____

_____

What items might the couple have now if they didn't have a child (children)?_____

_____

_____

_____

_____

_____

Biology of Heredity Review

Activity A

Chapter 4

Name _____

Date _____ Period_____

Heredity shapes many of a person's traits. You can understand how traits are passed on by studying the biology of heredity. Fill in the blanks in the story below. This will help you review the terms and concepts about heredity in your text.

Carlos began life with the union of an _____(1)_____ from his mother and a _____(2)_____ from his father. This beginning is called _____(3)_____. At that time, Carlos was just one _____(4)_____.

However, his _____(5)_____ contained a hereditary blueprint that determined how Carlos would look later in life. This set of instructions for building Carlos was carried in a chemical compound called _____(6)_____ , which is found in threadlike structures called chromosomes. Carlos was given _____(7)_____ of these when he was born. They contained _____(8)_____ that determined his traits.

Carlos is tall for his age and has light brown hair like his father. Like his mother, he has Rh negative, type B blood. Carlos inherited _____(9)_____ eyes because his mother's eyes are blue and his father's eyes are blue.

Carlos has 23 chromosomes in each of his _____(10)_____ cells. When his father's sperm and his mother's ovum united, a fertilized egg cell with _____(11)_____ chromosomes was formed. As the fertilized egg cell _____(12)_____ , each of Carlos' cells that formed had 23 pairs of chromosomes. One chromosome from each pair originated from each of Carlos' _____(13)_____ . During the course of nine months, this fertilized egg cell developed into a _____(14)_____ . The genes from each parent determined Carlos' unique _____(15)_____.

1. _____
2. _____
3. _____
4. _____
5. _____
6. _____
7. _____
8. _____
9. _____
10. _____
11. _____
12. _____
13. _____
14. _____
15. _____

Inheriting Unique Traits

Activity B   Name _____

Chapter 4   Date _____ Period _____

All people inherit half of their genes from their mother and half from their father. However, a child may be born with one or more traits that no one else in the family possesses. Invite a biology teacher to your class to discuss genetic mutations. Use the information provided to answer the questions below.

What is a mutation? _____

_____

_____

What causes mutations? _____

_____

_____

_____

Are changes from mutations always major? (Give examples to support your answer.) _____

_____

_____

_____

_____

_____

What are some examples of harmful or undesirable mutations? _____

_____

_____

_____

_____

_____

What are some examples of helpful or desirable mutations? _____

_____

_____

_____

_____

_____

_____

_____

_____

_____

Multiple Births

Activity C

Chapter 4

Name _____

Date _____ Period _____

Many parents-to-be and new parents have questions about multiple births. Pretend that you are a consultant who answers questions about pregnancy for a health clinic. Using information in your text, write your answers to the following questions.

Dear Sir or Madam,

My husband and I are thinking about starting a family, and we were wondering whether I might have twins. My grandmother and my great-great grandmother had twins. Does this mean that I have a good chance of having twins?

Sincerely,

Madeline Huttoz

Dear Mrs. Huttoz,

_____

_____

_____

_____

Dear Sir or Madam,

My wife gave birth to twins a month ago–a boy and a girl. They look so much alike now that my mother says they must be identical twins. How can we tell whether our twins are identical?

Sincerely,

Joseph Manuel

Dear Mr. Manuel,

_____

_____

_____

_____

Dear Sir or Madam,

I recently gave birth to triplets. Two are girls and they look exactly alike. The other is a boy, so I know all three cannot be identical. Is it possible to have two children that are identical and one that is fraternal, or could they all be fraternal?

Sincerely,

Kelly Willson

Dear Mrs. Willson,

_____

_____

_____

_____

Development in the Unborn

Activity D   Name _____

Chapter 4   Date _____ Period_____

Development before birth is more rapid than at any other time. Due to the many changes that occur, the unborn baby's development is divided into the germinal, embryonic, and fetal stages. Check the correct stage for each description.

Germinal Stage	*Embryonic Stage*	*Fetal Stage*	
_____	_____	_____	1. Fat is forming under the skin.
_____	_____	_____	2. One sperm has just penetrated an unfertilized egg.
_____	_____	_____	3. Limb buds, which will be arms and legs, are forming.
_____	_____	_____	4. Bone cells replace cartilage.
_____	_____	_____	5. Pregnancy becomes obvious to others.
_____	_____	_____	6. The egg begins to embed in the wall of the uterus.
_____	_____	_____	7. The age of viability is reached.
_____	_____	_____	8. The umbilical cord begins to function.
_____	_____	_____	9. A developing baby first resembles a small human being at this time.
_____	_____	_____	10. The zygote is one-third of the way down the fallopian tube.
_____	_____	_____	11. Body parts grow and mature.
_____	_____	_____	12. Head hair is appearing.
_____	_____	_____	13. Teeth are forming.
_____	_____	_____	14. Internal organs are developing.
_____	_____	_____	15. The amnion, placenta, and umbilical cord are beginning.
_____	_____	_____	16. Ears and eyes are beginning to form.
_____	_____	_____	17. Mother feels her baby's movements.
_____	_____	_____	18. Lanugo (down) is forming.
_____	_____	_____	19. Eyelids and nails are developing.
_____	_____	_____	20. Skin is developing.

Prenatal Care and Childbirth

5

Mothers-to-Be Affect the Health of Their Unborns

Activity A

Chapter 5

Name _____

Date _____ Period _____

A person's environment is always important to development, especially during the times of rapid change. A mother's body is the baby's environment during a time of rapid change. Thus, a mother's characteristics and health practices greatly affect the health of her baby. In the following list, mark a plus sign in front of maternal traits or health practices that help an unborn baby's health. Mark a minus sign in front of those practices that are harmful. Then choose one of the items listed and explain why it is helpful or harmful.

_____ happy and content with life in general

_____ has not had rubella or the vaccination

_____ relaxes in a sauna

_____ avoids even over-the-counter drugs

_____ sleeps well at night and takes naps during the day

_____ has a high-pressure job that causes various stress reactions

_____ has Rh + blood type and is married to a man with Rh – blood type

_____ is very underweight

_____ eats a well-balanced diet with a moderate caloric intake

_____ smokes moderately

_____ does not eat foods high in calcium

_____ has dental checkups

_____ exercises by walking

_____ is anemic

_____ is over 36 years of age

Trait or health practice chosen _____

Why does this help or harm the unborn? _____

_____

_____

_____

_____

_____

_____

_____

_____

_____

Menu for a Mother-to-Be

Activity B

Chapter 5

Name _____

Date _____ Period_____

Nutrition of a mother-to-be is important both before and during pregnancy. During the first three months of pregnancy, the unborn feeds on the nutrients from the yolk sac of the ovum and the mucous tissues that line the uterus. For the remaining six months before birth, the unborn receives nutrients through the umbilical cord. Using chart 5-5 of the text as a guideline, plan an appropriate three-day menu for a pregnant woman.

	Breakfast	Lunch	Dinner	Snacks
Day 1				
Day 2				
Day 3				

Drugs and Diseases in Mothers-to-Be

Activity C   Name _____

Chapter 5   Date _____ Period_____

Mothers-to-be can help prevent congenital problems in their babies by avoiding certain drugs and diseases during pregnancy. Do Internet research about the effects of one of the following during pregnancy and answer the questions below.

alcohol	high blood pressure	prescription medications
childhood illnesses	illegal drugs	sexually transmitted diseases
diabetes	over-the-counter drugs	smoking

1. What substance (drug or disease) did you choose to research? _____

2. List addresses of three Web sites you visited to research the substance's effect on unborn babies.

_____

_____

_____

3. Write a short paragraph describing what you learned about the effects of this substance on unborn babies when mothers are exposed to it during pregnancy.

_____

_____

_____

_____

_____

_____

_____

_____

4. What treatments are available for babies exposed to this substance prenatally? _____

_____

_____

_____

_____

5. What is the best advice you found in your search for helping pregnant women avoid this substance? _____

_____

_____

_____

_____

_____

The Role of the Father-to-Be in Pregnancy

Activity D

Chapter 5

Name _____

Date _____ Period _____

In the past, fathers-to-be were not able to take an active role in the birthing process. Many comic strips and comedy shows made fun of these fathers-to-be. Today, husbands can take a more active role in the birthing process. In the space below, mount or draw a cartoon that makes fun of the traditional role of the father-to-be. Then answer the question that follows.

How do the concepts in these drawings contrast with the role taken by fathers who are more involved in the birthing process? _____

_____

_____

_____

_____

_____

_____

_____

_____

_____

_____

_____

Choices for Delivery

Activity E

Chapter 5

Name _____

Date _____ Period_____

Parents-to-be have a number of choices as to where and how their child will be delivered. Before making a choice, they need to weigh the advantages and disadvantages of the many options. Complete the chart below by listing advantages and disadvantages of the following options concerning delivery.

	Advantages	Disadvantages
Home delivery		
Birthing room delivery		
Standard hospital delivery		
Natural childbirth		
Lamaze method		
Leboyer method		
C-section method		

Stages of Labor

Activity F

Chapter 5

Name _____

Date _____ Period_____

At some point during the final stage of pregnancy, labor begins. The process of labor allows the baby to move out of the mother's body. Labor is divided into three stages, which are shown below. In the space provided, label each stage and describe what happens during that stage.

Stage 1

Stage of labor _____

Events of the stage _____

_____

_____

_____

_____

_____

_____

_____

_____

Stage 2

Stage of labor _____

Events of the stage _____

_____

_____

_____

_____

_____

_____

_____

_____

Stage 3

Stage of labor _____

Events of the stage _____

_____

_____

_____

_____

_____

_____

_____

_____

The Newborn

6

Newborns and Parents Adapt

Activity A

Chapter 6

Name _____

Date _____ Period _____

Newborns must make many adaptations. Some of these adaptations are needed for life itself and must occur in the minutes after birth. Other changes occur within the four weeks of the neonatal stage. During the newborn stage, parents-to-be also must adapt to being parents. In the spaces provided, write descriptive phrases that depict the change from an unborn to a newborn status. (The example listed will help you get started.) Then list some suggestions to make the transition from prospective parenthood to parenthood easier.

Unborn	*Newborn*
From _____*being supplied oxygen*_____	to _____*needing to breathe to get oxygen*_____
From _____	to _____
From _____	to _____
From _____	to _____
From _____	to _____
From _____	to _____
From _____	to _____
From _____	to _____
From _____	to _____
From _____	to _____

Making the Change to Parenthood Easier

1. _____
_____
_____

2. _____
_____
_____

3. _____
_____
_____

Reflexes of the Newborn

Activity B

Chapter 6

Name _____

Date _____ Period _____

Reflexes are built-in behaviors. Checking the newborn's reflexes is a way for physicians to measure the maturity and health of the nervous system. Newborns have more reflexes than adults. Many reflexes disappear as a baby develops. Some are replaced by voluntary movements. For each of the eight examples of reflexes named in your text, describe the stimulus (what triggers the reflex), and the expected reaction. Using another source, give the name of an additional reflex, its stimulus, and the expected reaction. Then answer the questions that follow.

Rooting Reflex

Stimulus _____

Reaction _____

_____

_____

Palmar Reflex

Stimulus _____

Reaction _____

_____

_____

Plantar Reflex

Stimulus _____

Reaction _____

_____

_____

Babinski Reflex

Stimulus _____

Reaction _____

_____

_____

Moro Reflex

Stimulus _____

Reaction _____

_____

_____

(Continued)

Name_____

Walking Reflex

Stimulus_____

Reaction_____

_____

_____

Withdrawal Reflex

Stimulus_____

Reaction_____

_____

_____

Sucking Reflex

Stimulus_____

Reaction_____

_____

_____

(Name of reflex) _____

Stimulus_____

Reaction_____

_____

_____

1. Why are reflexes important in determining the health of the newborn's nervous system?_____

_____

_____

_____

2. What is an example of a reflex that is needed for survival? _____

_____

_____

_____

3. How can a reflex lead to a voluntary, learned behavior?_____

_____

_____

_____

Shopping for the Newborn

Activity C

Chapter 6

Name _____

Date _____ Period _____

Wise shopping for the newborn includes buying the needed clothing and selecting good quality. It also means finding the best buys. Practice shopping for a newborn in the following ways. (a) Record the price of two brands of each item. (b) Based on hangtag or package information, decide which brand you think is best and state the reason(s) for your choice. (c) Calculate the total cost.

Item 1: Cotton knit nightgowns or kimonos

Brand _____ Cost _____   Brand _____ Cost _____

Chosen brand _____   Reason(s) _____

_____

Item 2: Cotton knit shirts

Brand _____ Cost _____   Brand _____ Cost _____

Chosen brand _____   Reason(s) _____

_____

Item 3: Sweaters or sweatshirts

Brand _____ Cost _____   Brand _____ Cost _____

Chosen brand _____   Reason(s) _____

_____

Item 4: Knit cap

Brand _____ Cost _____   Brand _____ Cost _____

Chosen brand _____   Reason(s) _____

_____

Item 5: Diapers (cloth or disposable)

Brand _____ Cost _____   Brand _____ Cost _____

Chosen brand _____   Reason(s) _____

_____

Item 6: Plastic pants (if cloth diapers are chosen)

Brand _____ Cost _____   Brand _____ Cost _____

Chosen brand _____   Reason(s) _____

_____

(Continued)

Name_____

Item 7: Socks

Brand _____ Cost _____   Brand _____ Cost _____

Chosen brand _____   Reason(s) _____

_____

Item 8: Bibs

Brand _____ Cost _____   Brand _____ Cost _____

Chosen brand _____   Reason(s) _____

_____

Item 9: Dressy outfit

Brand _____ Cost _____   Brand _____ Cost _____

Chosen brand _____   Reason(s) _____

_____

Total Cost

4 nightgowns or kimonos	$ _____
4 knit shirts	_____
3 sweaters or sweatshirts	_____
1 cap	_____
3 dozen cloth diapers (or several boxes of disposables)	_____
3 plastic pants (if cloth diapers are used)	_____
4 pairs of socks	_____
6 bibs	_____
1 dressy outfit	_____
Total	$ _____

Learning Through the Senses

Activity D

Chapter 6

Name _____

Date _____ Period_____

Newborns come into the world able to see, hear, touch, taste, and smell. With each passing week, the senses of the newborn become more refined. The senses are one of the main ways in which people learn throughout life. In the space below, list what you have learned through each of your senses. Remember that some learnings are acquired through more than one sense. For example, people see and feel the shapes of objects.

1. See _*Shapes of objects;*_____

_____

_____

_____

_____

_____

2. Hear _____

_____

_____

_____

_____

_____

3. Feel _*Shapes of objects;*_____

_____

_____

_____

_____

_____

4. Taste _____

_____

_____

_____

_____

_____

5. Smell _____

_____

_____

_____

_____

_____

Toys for Newborns

Activity E   Name _____

Chapter 6   Date _____ Period_____

Newborns learn through their senses. Much of their learning comes from looking at toys and other objects. Even at such a young age, newborns show preferences for certain objects. Compare the pairs of drawings below. Choose the object that probably would be more appealing to a newborn. Then list some guidelines to use when choosing toys for newborns.

Object A	*Object B*	
		1. Newborn preference _____
		2. Newborn preference _____
		3. Newborn preference _____
		4. Newborn preference _____
		5. Newborn preference _____
		6. Newborn preference _____

List some guidelines for choosing toys for newborns. _____

_____

_____

_____

Meeting New Parents' Needs

Activity F

Chapter 6

Name _____

Date _____ Period_____

The first few weeks of caring for a baby are hard because new parents have so much to learn. New parents need to be organized so they have time to care for the baby, get enough rest, and spend some time away from the baby. In the space below, write some suggestions that will help new parents get organized and meet their own needs as well as the baby's. You may want to read some magazine articles or talk to parents of young children to get some ideas.

Helpful Hints for New Parents

1. _____
   _____
   _____

2. _____
   _____
   _____

3. _____
   _____
   _____

4. _____
   _____
   _____

5. _____
   _____
   _____

6. _____
   _____
   _____

7. _____
   _____
   _____

8. _____
   _____
   _____

9. _____
   _____
   _____

10. _____
   _____
   _____

Changes in Physical Growth

Activity A

Chapter 7

Name _____

Date _____ Period _____

The first few months of an infant's life are times of significant growth and change. In the spaces below, write words or phrases that describe skeletal growth in infants during the stages listed.

Length	Weight
1 month _____ _____ _____	1 month _____ _____ _____
6 months_____ _____ _____	6 months _____ _____ _____
1 year _____ _____ _____	1 year_____ _____ _____
Body Proportion	**Bones and Teeth**
1 month _____ _____ _____	1 month _____ _____ _____
6 months_____ _____ _____	6 months _____ _____ _____
1 year _____ _____ _____	1 year_____ _____ _____

Write a summary statement about an infant's physical growth._____

_____

_____

_____

Motor Skills Develop Rapidly

Activity B

Chapter 7

Name _____

Date _____ Period _____

Within one year, the almost helpless newborn becomes able (or almost able) to walk. He or she is also able to grasp the smallest object found on the floor. Age norms help adults to know when they can expect certain skills to emerge. Read each of the motor skills listed below. Then label them first, second, third, or fourth quarter (of the first year), according to when this skill usually emerges.

First quarter—age 1 month through 3 months

Second quarter—age 4 months through 6 months

Third quarter—age 7 months through 9 months

Fourth quarter—age 10 months through 12 months

Head-to-Foot Development

_____ 1. pulls to a stand

_____ 2. sits without support

_____ 3. holds chest up with arm support

_____ 4. holds chin up

_____ 5. stands with help of adult

_____ 6. creeps

_____ 7. sits with support

_____ 8. sits in high chair and grasps

_____ 9. stands while holding furniture

_____ 10. crawls

_____ 11. walks when led (cruising)

_____ 12. sits on lap and holds an object

Center-to-Extremities Development

_____ 13. grasps a nonmoving object

_____ 14. accepts two objects handed to him or her

_____ 15. swipes at objects with either hand

_____ 16. grasps dangling objects

_____ 17. grasps with thumb in opposition to fingers

_____ 18. brings objects grasped to mouth

_____ 19. requires adult support of his or her body to prevent swaying while attempting to grasp

_____ 20. accepts three objects handed to him or her

Observation: Babies Use Motor Skills in Play

Activity C   Name _____

Chapter 7   Date _____ Period_____

During the second half of the first year, infants demonstrate many motor skills in play. They use these skills to achieve certain goals of play, such as crawling after a rolling ball and picking it up. Observe a six-month-old to one-year-old playing in a good play environment. (The play environment should include enough space for the child to move around and several toys within reach.) Before you observe, become familiar with the following questions. Then answer the questions soon after observation.

1. Identifying information. Gender and age of baby in months and weeks_____

   Describe play space and toys _____

   _____

   _____

   _____

   _____

   Adults present_____

   _____

2. Was the baby's head steady? _____

   _____

   How did the baby use his or her head to help play? _____

   _____

   _____

3. Did the baby roll over?_____

   _____

   If the baby rolled over, describe the incident. _____

   _____

   _____

   _____

4. Did the baby sit?_____

   Did the baby need any support from others or did the baby use his or her own arms and hands?_____

   _____

   For what length of time did the baby sit? _____

   Did the baby topple over from the sitting position?_____

   If so, what may have been the cause? _____

   _____

   _____

5. Did the baby crawl? _____Creep? _____

   How far? _____

   Were the movements smooth? _____

   _____

(Continued)

Name_____

6. Did the baby pull up to a standing position? _____

About how many times?_____

What was used to aid the pull up? _____

How did the baby get down into a sitting position again?_____

_____

7. Did the baby take a few steps?_____

With or without support? _____

If the baby needed support, who or what provided the support?_____

If without support, how far did the baby walk? _____

8. What object did the baby try to grasp? _____

_____

9. Categorize the baby's grasping ability according to the chart 7-9 in textbook.

_____

_____

10. Summarize the baby's motor development by writing either *mastered, attempted,* or *not attempted* in the blanks beside the following skills:

_____   holding head steady when turning neck left or right

_____   rolling over

_____   sitting with support

_____   sitting without support

_____   crawling

_____   creeping

_____   pulling up

_____   returning to sitting position after pulling up

_____   walking with support

_____   walking without support

Intellectual Development of the Infant

Toys to Stimulate a Baby's Perception

Activity A

Chapter 8

Name _____

Date _____ Period _____

Babies' perceptions are stimulated when they have toys that are interesting. Using chart 8-3 of your text as a guide, select an appropriate toy for each of the four age groups. Complete the chart as you make your choices. Then answer the question that follows.

Age Group	Name of Toy	Brand	Reason(s) for Choice
Birth to 3 months			
3 to 6 months			
6 to 9 months			
9 to 12 months			

Why are toys important to an infant's intellectual development? _____

_____

_____

_____

_____

Mental Advances in the First Year

Activity B   Name _____

Chapter 8   Date _____ Period_____

During the first year, a baby's mental development advances quickly. Piaget has used four substages of the sensorimotor stage to describe the remarkable development. Place the letter of the correct substage in front of the following descriptive phrases.

Substages

a. Substage I: Practicing Reflexes (birth to 1 month)

b. Substage II: Repeating New Learnings (1 to 4 months)

c. Substage III: Beginning to Control Their World (4 to 8 months)

d. Substage IV: Applying Learnings to Solve Complex Problems (8 to 12 months)

Descriptive Phrases

_____   1. Baby plays with his or her own hands.

_____   2. Baby looks down after toy is thrown from high chair.

_____   3. Baby realizes there is a connection between what he or she did and what happened.

_____   4. Baby mouths, squeezes, hits, turns, and shakes an object trying to see what the object does.

_____   5. Baby sucks milk from breast or bottle with strong, steady movements.

_____   6. Baby cries, then listens, and repeats these actions until mother comes.

_____   7. Baby sucks his or her thumb.

_____   8. Baby tries blinking his or her eyes after seeing an adult play in this manner.

_____   9. Baby picks up toy that is partially hidden under a blanket.

_____   10. Baby starts sucking movements as soon as he or she is placed in a nursing position.

_____   11. Baby takes off box lid and gets toy out of the box.

_____   12. Baby shakes bed to make cradle gym bounce day after day.

_____   13. Baby grasps anything that touches his or her palm.

_____   14. Baby makes many different crying and other sounds.

_____   15. Baby grasps object held in front of him or her.

_____   16. Baby cries at a steady rate when clothes are removed.

_____   17. Baby hits an object softly, then hard, and listens for the change in sound.

_____   18. Baby puts a toy boat in a pool and pushes it across the water.

_____   19. Baby blinks when an object comes near his or her face.

_____   20. Baby looks for his or her mother when mother crouches behind the couch while the baby is looking.

Object Identity

Activity C

Chapter 8

Name _____

Date _____ Period_____

Object identity is a landmark in mental development. It allows humans to perceive a person or object to be the same even though contact is not continuous. Read the following story and answer the questions that follow.

Terence, a seven-month-old, has become very attached to his pacifier. His mother lost his pacifier while on an afternoon outing with Terence. Terence is ready for bed and wants his pacifier. His mother gives him a new pacifier that is the same kind as his old one. Terence sucks the pacifier for a minute. Then he drops the pacifier and begins to cry.

1. How did Terence know this was not his old pacifier? _____

_____

_____

2. Why might Terence react this way even though he was given the same kind of pacifier? _____

_____

_____

3. Would Terence know whether his mother or a different person was holding him? How do you know? _____

_____

_____

4. Which objects or people would likely have identity first in babies' lives? _____

_____

_____

_____

_____

5. How can object identity lead to joy? _____

_____

_____

_____

How can object identity lead to sadness?_____

_____

_____

_____

6. Why must a baby develop a concept of object permanence before he or she develops object identity? _____

_____

_____

_____

_____

Learning to Talk—A Complex Skill

Activity D

Chapter 8

Name _____

Date _____ Period _____

Talking is one of the most complex skills a person learns in development. Several skills must develop prior to a baby's saying those first words. For each of the pretalking skills below, suggest one or more ways adults may help the development of the skill and thus help the baby learn to talk.

Pretalking Skills	Ways to Help
Understands object permanence	
Understands that people, objects, places, and events have names	
Remembers words that go with people, objects, places, and events	
Is able to make the sounds needed to talk	
Sees talking as important	

Social-Emotional Development of the Infant

9

Difficult Babies Make Parenting Stressful

Activity A

Name _____

Chapter 9

Date _____ Period _____

Learning parenting skills is a hard job, even when life with baby goes smoothly. Sometimes the baby's difficult temperament makes parenting much more stressful. If an adult handles a difficult baby in negative ways, more stress for both adult and baby is likely. Positive responses to a difficult baby will relieve some of the adult's stress and may, over a long time, change a baby's responses. Read the following descriptions and write an example of how an adult may handle each situation in a positive way.

1. Jan was always a fretful sleeper. At first, her mother laughed, "Jan just has her days and nights mixed up." After a year of Jan's night owl ways, Jan's mother is feeling increased stress.

   Positive response suggestions _____

   _____

   _____

   _____

   _____

   _____

   _____

   _____

   _____

2. Tyrone's mother has worked almost since Tyrone was born 10 months ago. His mother picks him up at 5:30 p.m. from the child care center on the way home from her workplace. By 6:00 p.m., Tyrone's mother is busy preparing supper, which is served at 7:00 p.m. when Tyrone's father returns home. The time between 6:00 and 7:00 p.m. is never pleasant. Tyrone continuously frets, even though his mother hands him bites of food and a few toys.

   Positive response suggestions _____

   _____

   _____

   _____

   _____

   _____

   _____

   _____

   _____

(Continued)

Name_____

3. Sondra is an adorable baby as long as everything remains exactly the same in her life. Sondra's parents like to visit their parents on weekends, and the grandparents certainly look forward to time with Sondra. However, the weekends are disasters for Sondra and all the loving adults in her life. Sondra howls at night and has nothing to do with the new toys her grandparents spent hours selecting.

Positive response suggestions

_____

_____

_____

_____

_____

_____

_____

_____

4. Juan, who is eight months old, has never liked staying in his car seat. His protests have become more and more vocal. Juan's father, who takes him to a child care center on workdays, knows that Juan must stay in the car seat for safety reasons. Juan's father often wonders whether his son's crying will distract him as he drives.

Positive response suggestions

_____

_____

_____

_____

_____

_____

_____

_____

5. Debbie's mother is embarrassed. Her beautiful little girl always looks as though she has just finished crying or is about ready to start. Even when life is going smoothly, Debbie looks pouty. When life is less than smooth, one-year-old Debbie will react with such cries and resistance that people stop and stare. Debbie's mother wonders what people must think about her as a parent.

Positive response suggestions

_____

_____

_____

_____

_____

_____

_____

_____

Building a Trusting Relationship

Activity B

Chapter 9

Name _____

Date _____ Period _____

Building a trusting relationship between a loving adult and a child is important, because trust in one adult often gives a child a more general feeling of trust in others. Providing a consistent world seems to be the root of trust. In the chart below, give specific examples of how an adult can provide a consistent world for a baby. Then answer the questions that follow.

Areas of Consistency	Examples
Physical needs are met.	
Psychological needs are met.	
Needs are met each time.	
Environment remains somewhat the same.	

1. How can a caregiver's feelings affect a baby's trust in that caregiver? _____

_____

_____

2. How can developing trust affect a person in adult life?_____

_____

_____

3. How can developing mistrust affect a person in adult life?_____

_____

_____

Observation: Attachment Behaviors

Activity C

Chapter 9

Name _____

Date _____ Period_____

Babies form intense feelings for their main caregivers. Because babies cannot say "I love you" in words, they show their dependence and love through many attachment behaviors. Later, babies express loving feelings for other adults, children, and even pets and toys. Observe a one-year-old baby with an important adult in his or her life and ask the adult questions about the baby's attachment. Then provide the following information.

1. Age of baby _____   Gender _____

   Relationship of adult to baby (mother, father, other) _____

2. How did the baby try to stay close to the adult? _____

   _____

   _____

   _____

   _____

   _____

3. What "I love you" signals did the baby send to the adult? _____

   _____

   _____

   _____

   _____

   _____

   _____

4. When did the adult first notice the baby's attachment behaviors?_____

   _____

   _____

   _____

   _____

   _____

5. According to the adult, when are these attachment behaviors the most intense? _____

   _____

   _____

   _____

   _____

   _____

(Continued)

Name_____

6. Who are other important adults in the baby's life, and how does the baby show loving feelings to each of them?

a. _____

_____

_____

b. _____

_____

_____

c. _____

_____

_____

d. _____

_____

_____

7. Is the baby close to other children? If so, what is their relationship to the baby (brother, sister, other)? How does the baby show them loving feelings?_____

_____

_____

_____

_____

_____

_____

_____

8. Does the baby seem attached to a pet, one or more toys, or a security object, such as a pacifier or blanket? Explain. _____

_____

_____

_____

_____

_____

_____

_____

_____

Helping to Ease Separation Anxiety

Activity D

Chapter 9

Name _____

Date _____ Period_____

Ten- to twelve-month-old babies will often cry when adults they love leave them with other adults. Crying babies often make adults feel concerned and guilty. The feelings of the adults are especially intense when babies who have gone readily to sitters in the past *suddenly* seem upset. In the space below, write some suggestions for adults to help relieve separation anxiety. Cite any facts that help to explain why your suggestions will help.

_____

_____

_____

_____

_____

_____

_____

_____

_____

_____

_____

_____

_____

_____

_____

_____

_____

_____

_____

_____

_____

_____

_____

_____

_____

_____

_____

_____

_____

Foods Babies Should Not Eat

Activity A

Chapter 10

Name _____

Date _____ Period_____

Many adult foods are unsafe for babies. Beside each item listed, write the reason the food (or foods) should be considered unsafe for babies.

Food	Reason
Alcohol	
Berries and grapes	
Caffeine-free soft drinks	
Cake, cookies, and candy, in excess	
Carrot, raw	
Cocoa, coffee, soft drinks, and tea	
Crackers, in excess	
Fruit drinks, artificially flavored	
Hot dogs, sliced in rounds	
Nuts, raisins, and popcorn	
Unpasteurized yogurt and yeast	

Choices in Baby Foods

Activity B

Chapter 10

Name _____

Date _____ Period_____

Although commercially prepared juices, cereals, fruits, vegetables, meats, and other foods are available for babies, many adults have become concerned about some additives in baby food products. For this reason as well as others, many adults have been preparing baby foods in their home. Once the baby begins eating solid foods, the adult must make a choice in baby foods. The following activity will help you see some of the factors to consider when choosing baby foods. Using a cookbook containing baby food recipes, prepare a fruit, a vegetable, and a meat for a baby. In the spaces below, compare the homemade food with a similar food that was commercially prepared. Then, after skimming through some other recipes, answer the questions that follow.

Fruit

Type _____

Method of preparation _____

_____

_____

_____

_____

Preparation time _____

Cost of ingredients _____

_____

Cost per ounce (homemade) _____

Cost per ounce (commercially prepared) _____

_____

Vegetable

Type _____

Method of preparation _____

_____

_____

_____

_____

Preparation time _____

Cost of ingredients _____

_____

Cost per ounce (homemade) _____

Cost per ounce (commercially prepared) _____

_____

(Continued)

Name_____

Meat

Type _____

Method of preparation _____

_____

_____

_____

_____

_____

Preparation time _____

Cost of ingredients _____

_____

_____

Cost per ounce (homemade) _____

Cost per ounce (commercially prepared) _____

_____

1. What types of appliances or kitchen tools are needed to make baby foods? _____

_____

_____

_____

2. How available are baby food recipe books, and what are their costs? _____

_____

_____

_____

3. How do the types of foods available commercially compare with the types that can be prepared at home?

_____

_____

_____

4. How do the storage requirements of commercially prepared foods compare with those of homemade foods?

_____

_____

_____

5. How do commercially prepared and homemade foods compare in terms of nutrients and additives?

_____

_____

_____

6. If you were responsible for feeding a baby, which type of food would you use? Explain your answer.

_____

_____

_____

_____

_____

_____

Wise Clothing Choices

Activity C

Chapter 10

Name _____

Date _____ Period_____

Babies' clothing should fit their needs. Wise choices in clothing can make babies safer, more comfortable, and freer to move and learn. Wise choices are also good consumer practices. Select three garments to rate. Using chart 10-11 of your text and other text information, rate each garment by circling appropriate points on each scale. Share the reasons for your ratings with class members.

Garment 1 (type) _____

Brief description _____

_____

_____

Ratings

	1	2	3	4	5
Safety	very safe				not safe
Comfort	very comfortable				not comfortable
Care	easy				difficult
Allowance for Growth	much				none

(Continued)

Name_____

Garment 2 (type)_____

Brief description _____

_____

_____

Ratings

Safety	1 very safe	2	3	4	5 not safe
Comfort	1 very comfortable	2	3	4	5 not comfortable
Care	1 easy	2	3	4	5 difficult
Allowance for Growth	1 much	2	3	4	5 none

Garment 3 (type)_____

Brief description _____

_____

_____

Ratings

Safety	1 very safe	2	3	4	5 not safe
Comfort	1 very comfortable	2	3	4	5 not comfortable
Care	1 easy	2	3	4	5 difficult
Allowance for Growth	1 much	2	3	4	5 none

Play Throughout the House

Activity D

Chapter 10

Name _____

Date _____ Period_____

Collect or make three sets of toys for a baby. (Examples could be sets for kitchen play, bath play, and ball play.). Place each set of toys in a suitable container, such as a box, plastic pail, or dishpan. Have your teacher check the toys and container for safety. Describe your toys and container in the chart below.

Then ask a parent of a baby between 7 and 12 months of age to use the three sets of toys with the baby for a couple of weeks. After this time, interview the parents using the questions below the chart. Record their responses and share your findings with the class.

Set	Toys Selected	Container
1		
2		
3		

1. Age of baby who played with toys _____

2. Gender of baby who played with toys _____

3. Evaluation of Set 1 toys:

   Did the baby seem to enjoy the toys? _____

   Which toys did the baby play with most? _____

   _____

   How did the baby play with the toys (such as mouthing, stacking, hitting with them)?_____

   _____

   _____

   _____

   _____

   Was the container easy for the baby to handle?_____

   Did the baby also use the container as a toy? _____

(Continued)

Name_____

4. Evaluation of Set 2 toys:

   Did the baby seem to enjoy the toys? _____

   Which toys did the baby play with most? _____

   _____

   How did the baby play with the toys (such as mouthing, stacking, hitting with them)?_____

   _____

   _____

   _____

   _____

   Was the container easy for the baby to handle?_____

   Did the baby also use the container as a toy? _____

5. Evaluation of Set 3 toys:

   Did the baby seem to enjoy the toys? _____

   Which toys did the baby play with most? _____

   _____

   How did the baby play with the toys (such as mouthing, stacking, hitting with them)?_____

   _____

   _____

   _____

   _____

   Was the container easy for the baby to handle?_____

   Did the baby also use the container as a toy? _____

6. What toys or containers would you change, if any? _____

   _____

7. Which of the baby's toy preferences surprised you? _____

   _____

   _____

8. How did the parent respond to your project?_____

   _____

   _____

   _____

   _____

How's the Baby-Adult Interaction?

Activity E   Name _____

Chapter 10   Date _____ Period_____

Through informal observation, you can learn much about baby-adult interaction. Choose two of the following places to observe: grocery store; mall; child care center (at drop-off or pick-up times); restaurant or fast-food place; sports event or recreational activity; or other public place (such as a library, park, bus, or train). Look for a parent with an infant and informally watch them interact. Do not talk to or get involved with the adult or baby. Then write your observations and reactions in the space provided below.

1. Setting: _____

   Description of baby and adult: _____

   _____

   _____

   _____

   Observation: _____

   _____

   _____

   _____

   _____

   Reaction to adult-child interaction: _____

   _____

   _____

   _____

2. Setting: _____

   Description of baby and adult: _____

   _____

   _____

   _____

   Observation: _____

   _____

   _____

   _____

   _____

   Reaction to adult-child interaction: _____

   _____

   _____

   _____

Growth Slows and Slows

Activity A

Chapter 11

Name _____

Date _____ Period_____

Babies grow rapidly in the first year, but their growth slows some in the toddler years. Plot the length/height norms and the weight norms for the first, second, and third years of life. Refer to charts 11-2, 11-4, and 7-1 in your text. Then join the dots on each graph to see the growth pattern.

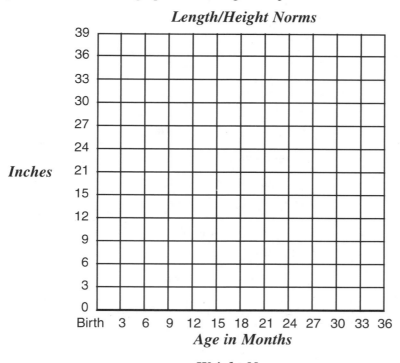

Length/Height Norms

Inches

Age in Months

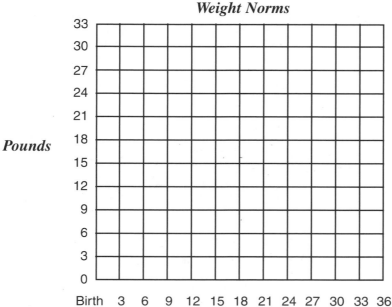

Weight Norms

Pounds

Age in Months

Motor Skills Continue to Develop

Activity B

Chapter 11

Name _____

Date _____ Period_____

During the toddler years, many gross-motor and fine-motor skills, which were learned in the first year, are refined. Many new motor skills also emerge. Age norms help adults know the order in which certain motor skills will emerge and the approximate age in which the skills most often occur.

Gross-Motor Skills

Describe the typical toddler motor skills by writing the letters **RS** (for refined skill) or **NS** (for new skill) beside each motor skill.

_____ 1. walking

_____ 2. running

_____ 3. jumping

_____ 4. climbing

_____ 5. throwing

_____ 6. catching

Match the age ranges below to the motor skills.

Age Ranges

A. before one year of age

B. 12 to 17 months of age

C. 18 to 24 months of age

D. 24 to 36 months of age

Skills

_____ 7. walking with an upright stance

_____ 8. stepping off of low objects

_____ 9. jumping off of low objects with two feet

_____ 10. climbing on chairs

_____ 11. throwing accidentally

_____ 12. catching by squatting down and picking up an object

_____ 13. bending at the waist to catch an object

Fine-Motor Skills

Describe the typical toddler motor skills by writing the letters **RS** (for refined skill) or **NS** (for new skill) beside each motor skill.

_____ 1. holding an object between thumb and index finger

_____ 2. holding spoon for self-feeding

_____ 3. removing some clothing

_____ 4. holding crayons between thumb and fingers

_____ 5. showing some hand preference

Match the age ranges and the motor skills.

Age Ranges

A. before one year of age

B. 12 to 17 months of age

C. 18 to 24 months of age

D. 24 to 36 months of age

Skills

_____ 6. holding an object between the thumb and index finger

_____ 7. opening doors by turning a knob

_____ 8. holding crayon in fist

_____ 9. hitting pegs with a hammer

_____ 10. inserting large objects in holes

_____ 11. stringing large beads

Motor Skills of a Toddler on the Go

Activity C   Name _____

Chapter 11   Date _____ Period_____

Toddlers are all different, but their most common physical characteristic is that they are constantly on the go. As toddlers move, they refine old motor skills and learn new motor skills. Observe a toddler between the ages of 12 and 35 months in a play situation. Then complete the following record.

1. Age of toddler _____ months   Gender _____

   Physical environment (inside or outside, toys, objects to climb onto or to jump off)_____

   _____

   _____

   Others present (children and adults)_____

   _____

2. For each of the following skills employed by the toddler, describe the level of the skill and what the toddler was doing or trying to do while using the skill.

   Walking_____

   _____

   _____

   _____

   Running_____

   _____

   _____

   _____

   Jumping_____

   _____

   _____

   _____

   Climbing _____

   _____

   _____

   _____

   Throwing and catching _____

   _____

   _____

   _____

   _____

(Continued)

Name_____

3. Describe any fine-motor skills the toddler uses. _____

_____

_____

_____

_____

_____

_____

Did the toddler show hand preference?_____ If not, which activities were done

with the right hand? _____

Which activities were done with the left hand? _____

_____

4. After comparing your observations with the description in the text, how would you describe the general level
   of the toddler's gross-motor skills? _____

_____

_____

_____

_____

How would you describe the general level of the toddler's fine-motor skills? _____

_____

_____

_____

_____

_____

_____

_____

_____

Toddlers Are Scientists

Activity A

Chapter 12

Name _____

Date _____ Period_____

Toddlers have a need to find answers and solve problems. They are like natural scientists in many ways. In the space below, list some traits of scientists. (You may need to interview a science teacher or other scientists in order to list the traits.) Observe a toddler in play. Across from each trait of scientists, record one or more examples of similar traits you see in the toddler.

Traits of Scientists

Examples of Similar Traits in Toddlers

_____   _____
_____   _____
_____   _____
_____   _____
_____   _____
_____   _____
_____   _____
_____   _____
_____   _____
_____   _____
_____   _____
_____   _____
_____   _____
_____   _____
_____   _____
_____   _____
_____   _____
_____   _____
_____   _____
_____   _____
_____   _____
_____   _____
_____   _____
_____   _____

Toddlers Learn by Throwing Objects

Activity B

Chapter 12

Name _____

Date _____ Period_____

Toddlers seem to spend a lot of time throwing objects. Adults who care for toddlers spend countless hours picking up objects thrown from high chairs and over playpens and gates. Many adults wonder whether the toddler throws objects just to see how many times the adult will pick up the objects. The toddler cannot keep a time log or a score sheet. However, a toddler learns a great deal about objects by throwing them. Through the eyes and hands of a toddler, think about throwing different objects. What are toddlers learning? In the space below, list as many learnings as you can.

1. _____
2. _____
3. _____
4. _____
5. _____
6. _____
7. _____
8. _____
9. _____
10. _____
11. _____
12. _____
13. _____
14. _____
15. _____
16. _____
17. _____
18. _____
19. _____
20. _____

Toys Are Tools for Thinking

Activity C

Chapter 12

Name _____

Date _____ Period _____

Toys are needed for thinking. Almost anything can become a toy to a toddler—a purchased toy, a cardboard box, pots and pans, an adult's face, and a piece of food. All toys help toddlers learn the properties of objects, such as color, texture, and size. Toys also help toddlers learn what happens when toys roll or sound when shaken. In the space below, list some of the learnings that may come from playing with four toys. Complete the chart with a fifth toy of your choice.

Toy	Toddler's Learnings	
	Properties	**What Happens**
Push/pull toy		
Cracker (food)		
Cardboard box		
Ball		
Your choice of toy:		

Toddlers Begin to Think

Activity D

Chapter 12

Name _____

Date _____ Period _____

According to Piaget, toddlers begin to think with their minds rather than their actions, between the first and second birthdays. Adults are often aware of toddlers' growing mental abilities. Interview a child care worker who works with 15- to 24-month-olds. Ask him or her to discuss the kinds of thinking skills toddlers display. Use the child care worker's examples to fill in examples of each category in the chart below.

Toddler Actions That Show Thinking Skills	
Achieving a goal	Making something work without being shown how
Imitating actions	Using words (correctly and incorrectly)

Social-Emotional Development of the Toddler

Toddlers View Themselves Through Adults

Activity A

Chapter 13

Name _____

Date _____ Period_____

Developing self-awareness is a process that begins at birth and continues throughout life. To a great extent, a person's self-awareness depends on how others react to him or her—whether in positive or negative ways. Toddlers have broader social relations and are better able to understand the reactions of others than are infants. Because of this, the toddler stage is highly important for developing self-awareness. After reading about each of the following situations, use the space below to describe the picture the toddler may be developing of himself or herself.

Situation	Toddler's Picture of Himself or Herself
Sarah was trying to help her mother with the dishes when a glass slipped from her hand and broke. Sarah's mother cleaned up the glass, smiled, and said, "Let me put away the glasses while you put the knives, forks, and spoons in the drawer."	
When the babysitter called to say she could not care for Carter as planned, Carter's mother took him shopping. She told Carter to keep his hands by his sides. In a gift and card store, he spotted a cute teddy bear. He asked his mother to let him hold it, but she ignored him. As he reached for the bear, Carter upset a small file box. The store owner picked up the spilled cards and handed Carter the bear. Carter's mother yelled at her son, "I told you to keep your hands down. You never mind me!"	
Taylor was twisting and turning as her parents tried to complete the initial office visit form at a doctor's office. Taylor's infant brother had a high fever and was fussy. After telling Taylor several times to stop moving, her father pointed his finger at her and said, "The police get naughty girls."	
Emmett had gotten into many things throughout the day, causing his mother extra cleaning tasks. At the evening meal, Emmett heard his mother say, "Emmett needs a drawer for holding his things. We could tape his picture to the drawer, so he'll know which one is his."	

(Continued)

Name_____

Situation	Toddler's Picture of Himself or Herself
Felicia's teenage sister was helping her get dressed. Felicia wanted to put on her shoes, but she couldn't get them on by herself. Felicia's sister said, "I'll pull and you push a little, and the shoe will go on." After the shoe was on, Felicia's sister said, "Thanks for the help. Helping each other is fun."	
While Leroy was turning the pages in a family photo album, he tore a page at the spiral binding. His parents said angrily, "Why are you so clumsy?" They jerked the book away from him.	
Mary was trying to help with the laundry. Mary's mother did not see her drop a new white blouse in the clothes washer with the load of jeans. The blouse came out of the washer looking dingy with a piece of its lace torn by a jean zipper. Mary's mother said, "The next time we wash, I'll show you which clothes you may put in the water. Then we will be careful not to put other clothes in the clothes washer."	
LaTanya put her pillow on the bed each morning as her mother made the bed. Her mother always said, "That's nice," as she redid the way LaTanya placed the pillow.	
Barbara's table manners left much to be desired by adult standards. Her father began to call her "Miss Piggy," which made everyone look at Barbara and laugh.	
Adolfo never wanted to go to bed at night. He would cry, "I NOT sleepy. No bed." His parents knew he wanted to stay in the family room and watch television. However, his parents knew he needed to sleep. Adolfo's parents would say, "Of course big boys are not sleepy. You may look at your books in bed." In 15 to 30 minutes, Adolfo was asleep.	

Toddlers Are Being Socialized

Activity B

Chapter 13

Name _____

Date _____ Period_____

Every toddler is being socialized, and every older child and adult who has contact with a toddler takes part in the process. Through socialization, a child gains those qualities needed for successful relationships with others. Match the following qualities through socialization with the appropriate examples. In some cases, more than one answer may be correct. Then answer the question that follows.

Qualities

A. ambition

B. concern for others

C. knowledge

D. self-control

E. skill

F. taste

Examples

_____ 1. Thirty-month-old Juan carefully pours a cup of water into the family puppy's dish.

_____ 2. Kim watches her mother as she fastens Kim's seat belt and then her own. Kim then imitates her mother's words, "All snug and safe."

_____ 3. Kelcy and his mother applaud the performers in a youth concert.

_____ 4. Keith's father always answers Keith's often-repeated question, "Whazzat?"

_____ 5. Yolanda's parents never yell at her when she spills milk at the table.

_____ 6. Kelly watches his father read his "big school books" almost every night.

_____ 7. James and his parents carry soup and some fruit to a neighbor who has been hurt in a fall.

_____ 8. Frank is shown how to get the stool and work the light switch in his room.

_____ 9. Maria and her mother "read" many stories together.

_____ 10. Michael's father always says "please" and "thank you" when he speaks to Michael.

What are some ways in which you might help socialize children in relationship to the qualities listed above?

_____

_____

_____

_____

_____

_____

_____

_____

_____

_____

Helping Toddlers Gain Self-Esteem

Activity C

Chapter 13

Name _____

Date _____ Period _____

Toddlers are striving to become independent and have others accept them as they are. In their efforts to be independent, toddlers often become stubborn or make mistakes. At these times, toddlers need firm kindness and acceptance from adults. With a group of other students in your class, plan and perform a skit that shows how adults can make toddlers lose or gain self-esteem. Choose a situation in which a toddler becomes stubborn or makes a mistake as the basis for the skit. Act out the situation and have the adult or adults involved react in a way that causes the toddler to lose self-esteem. Then, using the same basis, have the adult or adults react in a way that causes the toddler to gain self-esteem. Use the space provided to plan your ideas for the skit.

Characters _____

_____

_____

Basis for skit (toddler's stubborn action or mistake) _____

_____

_____

_____

Basic plot of portion in which adult actions lessen a toddler's self-esteem_____

_____

_____

_____

_____

_____

_____

_____

_____

Basic plot of portion in which adult actions increase a toddler's self-esteem _____

_____

_____

_____

_____

_____

_____

_____

_____

_____

Observation: Toddlers and Separation Anxiety

Activity D

Chapter 13

Name _____

Date _____ Period_____

Separation anxiety, the concern the young child has when separated from a main caregiver, peaks in the toddler years. Unlike the infant, the toddler is often aware of events leading to separation, such as parent(s) getting dressed for work. Toddlers, as compared with infants, also can be louder in their protests and often attempt to follow the main caregiver. Toddlers' reactions during their reunions with main caregivers vary from showing much pleasure to "ignoring" the returning adults, as though punishing them.

Observe two toddlers and adults during separation and reunion at any group program. In the space below, record the age and gender of each child. Then write a description of (a) the toddlers' and adults' (main caregiver and new caregiver) behaviors during separation, (b) the toddlers' and new caregivers' behaviors for 10 to 15 minutes after separation, (c) the toddlers' and main caregivers' behaviors during the reunion.

Toddler Age and Gender	Behaviors as Separation Begins	Behaviors after Main Caregiver Leaves	Behaviors During Reunion
Toddler 1:			
Toddler 2:			

Temper Tantrums and Toddlers

Activity E

Chapter 13

Name _____

Date _____ Period_____

Temper tantrums and toddlers seem to go together. Temper tantrums happen because events do not always go the way toddlers want them to and because toddlers have not learned other ways to express their anger. As toddlers grow older, temper tantrums become less common. In the space below, list events that might cause anger in a toddler and events that might cause anger in a high school student. Then compare ways in which toddlers and high school students might express their anger.

Causes of Anger	
In Toddlers	**In High School Students**

Expressions of Anger	
In Toddlers	**In High School Students**

How is anger different for toddlers and high school students? _____

_____

_____

How is anger similar for toddlers and high school students?_____

_____

_____

Bedtime Rituals

Activity A

Chapter 14

Name _____

Date _____ Period _____

Bedtime is often a dreaded time for toddlers who are tired and irritable; want to be where the action is; and may fear the dark, monsters, or nightmares. A pleasant, unhurried time with a parent before being left alone to sleep is comforting, especially when this time becomes a ritual. Plan a bedtime ritual for a toddler to be used for three nights. Be creative. Write your ideas in specific terms. For instance, list ideas for talking or quiet water play for each night, or list specific stories and/or songs you select. (Before beginning your plans, you may consult with a parent concerning some of the toddler's preferences.) Then ask a parent to try your plans for three nights and report how the toddler accepts the ritual. Also, have the parent report any suggestions for changes.

Bedtime Ritual

Toddler's first name _____ Age _____ Gender _____

Ritual Ideas	Parent's Comments and Suggestions

Toilet Learning

Activity B   Name _____

Chapter 14   Date _____ Period_____

Toilet learning is an important step in becoming independent and in being able to take part in many social activities. Toilet learning is a long process that requires the adults involved to be patient and understanding. When toddlers have problems with toilet learning, parents can feel stress, which in turn makes the toddler feel more stress. In the space below, write 10 tips for making toilet learning easier and less stressful for adults and toddlers.

1. _____
_____
_____

2. _____
_____
_____

3. _____
_____
_____

4. _____
_____
_____

5. _____
_____
_____

6. _____
_____
_____

7. _____
_____
_____

8. _____
_____
_____

9. _____
_____
_____

10. _____
_____
_____

Learning Happens in Everyday Experiences

Activity C

Chapter 14

Name _____

Date _____ Period_____

Toddlers' growing concepts are mainly learned through routine activities in the home and are practiced in play. Review the discussion in your text concerning toddler learnings that can take place during meals. (The discussion is found under the heading "Intellectual Needs.") In the space that follows, list concepts that toddlers can develop while bathing and dressing. Also give ideas concerning what adults can say or do to help the toddler develop these concepts.

Concepts Toddlers Can Learn While Bathing	
Concepts	**Ways Adults May Help**

(Continued)

Name_____

Concepts Toddlers Can Learn While Dressing	
Concepts	**Ways Adults May Help**

Planned Activities for Sensory Stimulation

Activity D

Chapter 14

Name _____

Date _____ Period_____

Select one activity from the sensory stimulation activities in this chapter. You also may select one of your own. Prepare to use the activity with toddlers by collecting any equipment needed and writing out the procedure you will use. Try each activity with a different toddler, or try each activity with the same toddler on a different day. (If time is a problem, work in groups of four and have each group member try one activity. Each member should then share his or her results with the group.)

Sensory Stimulation Activities

Preparation

Activity chosen _____

Expected learning _____

Supplies needed_____

_____

Procedure (include specific words you will use, movements, etc.) _____

_____

_____

_____

_____

Results

Toddler's first name _____ Age _____ Gender _____

Toddler's actions during activity_____

_____

_____

_____

_____

Did the activity appear to hold the toddler's interest? _____

Did the toddler appear to learn what was expected? Explain. _____

_____

Were any other learnings observed? Explain._____

_____

List any changes you would make if you used this activity with a toddler again._____

_____

_____

_____

_____

_____

Planned Activities for Problem Solving

Activity E   Name _____

Chapter 14   Date _____ Period_____

Try one problem-solving activity with a toddler. Record your results.

Problem-Solving Activities

Preparation

Activity chosen _____

Expected learning _____

Supplies needed_____

_____

Procedure (include specific words you will use, movements, etc.) _____

_____

_____

_____

_____

Results

Toddler's first name _____ Age _____ Gender _____

Toddler's actions during activity_____

_____

_____

_____

_____

Did the activity appear to hold the toddler's interest? _____

Did the toddler appear to learn what was expected? Explain. _____

_____

Were any other learnings observed? Explain._____

_____

List any changes you would make if you used this activity with a toddler again._____

_____

_____

_____

_____

_____

_____

Planned Motor Activities

Activity F

Chapter 14

Name _____

Date _____ Period_____

Try one motor activity with a toddler. Record your results.

Motor Activities

Preparation

Activity chosen _____

Expected learning _____

Supplies needed_____

_____

Procedure (include specific words you will use, movements, etc.) _____

_____

_____

_____

_____

Results

Toddler's first name _____ Age _____ Gender _____

Toddler's actions during activity_____

_____

_____

_____

_____

Did the activity appear to hold the toddler's interest? _____

Did the toddler appear to learn what was expected? Explain. _____

_____

Were any other learnings observed? Explain._____

_____

List any changes you would make if you used this activity with a toddler again._____

_____

_____

_____

_____

_____

_____

Modeling Language for Toddlers

Activity G

Chapter 14

Name _____

Date _____ Period_____

After age two, most toddlers begin to use language for talking with others and for thinking. Because language is learned mainly through imitation, adults must carefully model language for toddlers. After each description of a toddler's language, write the purpose for modeling the language. The purpose can be to (a) correct pronunciation, (b) correct grammar, (c) add a new word to vocabulary, or (d) correct meaning. Then restate the sentence in a way that reflects the purpose to the toddler.

1. Description: "I *ranned* to the barn."

    Purpose _____

    Restated sentence _____

2. Description: "I want my *piddah* on my bed!"

    Purpose _____

    Restated sentence _____

3. Description: "The apples *is* sweet."

    Purpose _____

    Restated sentence _____

4. Description: "See the *chicken* swim."

    Purpose _____

    Restated sentence _____

5. Description: "See my *foots*."

    Purpose _____

    Restated sentence _____

6. Description: "The kite *goes*."

    Purpose _____

    Restated sentence _____

7. Description: "I like *woses* in the garden."

    Purpose _____

    Restated sentence _____

8. Description: "Look at the man playing the *jello.*"

    Purpose _____

    Restated sentence _____

9. Description: "Daddy has *feathers* on his chin."

    Purpose _____

    Restated sentence _____

10. Description: "*Me* want to go."

    Purpose _____

    Restated sentence _____

Planned Language Activities

Activity H

Chapter 14

Name _____

Date _____ Period _____

Try one language activity with a toddler. Record your results.

Language Activities

Preparation

Activity chosen _____

Expected learning _____

Supplies needed _____

_____

Procedure (include specific words you will use, movements, etc.) _____

_____

_____

_____

_____

Results

Toddler's first name _____ Age _____ Gender _____

Toddler's actions during activity _____

_____

_____

_____

_____

Did the activity appear to hold the toddler's interest? _____

Did the toddler appear to learn what was expected? Explain. _____

_____

Were any other learnings observed? Explain. _____

_____

List any changes you would make if you used this activity with a toddler again. _____

_____

_____

_____

_____

_____

Transition Stages Are Difficult

Activity I

Chapter 14

Name _____

Date _____ Period_____

Toddlers enter a transition stage in which they still depend on others, and yet they need and want to be more independent. It is difficult for adults to meet both needs. As a result, the stage is not only a stressful period for the toddler but for the caring adult, as well. Some child development experts see similarities between the toddler's transition stage and the transition stage between being a teen and a young adult. In the space below, describe (with examples) how a teen and the adults in his or her life have conflicts during this transition period. Compare these to the types of conflicts toddlers have with adults during their transition period.

_____

_____

_____

_____

_____

_____

_____

_____

_____

_____

_____

_____

_____

_____

_____

_____

_____

_____

_____

_____

_____

_____

_____

_____

_____

_____

_____

Planned Activities for Self-Awareness

Activity J

Chapter 14

Name _____

Date _____ Period _____

Try a self-awareness activity with a toddler. Record your results.

Preparation

Activity chosen _____

Expected learning _____

Supplies needed_____

_____

Procedure (include specific words you will use, movements, etc.) _____

_____

_____

_____

_____

Results

Toddler's first name _____ Age _____ Gender _____

Toddler's actions during activity_____

_____

_____

_____

_____

Did the activity appear to hold the toddler's interest? _____

Did the toddler appear to learn what was expected? Explain. _____

_____

Were any other learnings observed? Explain._____

_____

List any changes you would make if you used this activity with a toddler again._____

_____

_____

_____

_____

_____

Average Heights and Weights of Preschoolers

Activity A

Chapter 15

Name _____

Date _____ Period _____

There is a steady increase in the height and weight of preschoolers. Plot the height norms and the weight norms for three-, four-, and five-year-olds. Next, join the dots on each graph to see the growth pattern. Plot the weights and heights of boys and girls in different colors and note any differences.

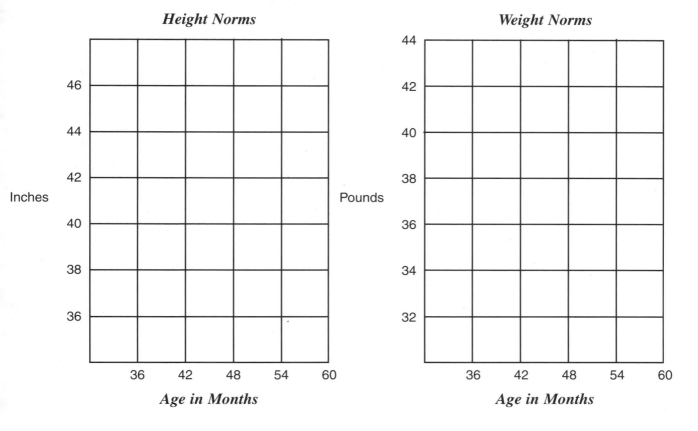

Height Norms

Inches

Age in Months

Weight Norms

Pounds

Age in Months

Preschoolers' Bodies Mature

Activity B   Name _____

Chapter 15   Date _____ Period_____

As preschool children's bodies mature, their body proportions become more like those of adults. Their organ systems also mature, especially by the end of the preschool years. Of course, there are differences in preschool children's physical development. Not all children mature at the same rate. Norms or averages are used as a point of comparison between a certain child and the "average" child. In the space below, supply descriptive phrases that depict the developmental norms of preschool children.

Brain _____   Head _____

_____   _____

Trunk _____   Bones _____

_____   _____

Heart _____   Teeth_____

_____   _____

Fat _____   Breathing _____

_____   _____

Legs _____   Abdomen _____

_____   _____

Chest/Waist/Hip Measurements < (30 months)   Digestive tract _____

(5 years)   _____

Height < (girls) 5 years   Weight < (girls) 5 years

(boys) 5 years   (boys) 5 years

Observation: Strength and Coordination Increase

Activity C

Chapter 15

Name _____

Date _____ Period_____

Compared with those of the toddler, the gross-motor skills for preschoolers are much more mature. Preschoolers' strength and coordination increase with each year, too. Choose an outdoor play setting to observe preschoolers, such as a backyard, a park, or a school playground. Equipment needs to be available for climbing (preferably both steps and a ladder) and for throwing. A balance beam is optional equipment. Observe two preschoolers, one who is three to three-and-one-half years old and the other who is five to five-and-one-half years old. List descriptive phrases for each child that depict their voluntary movements. It is best to watch these movements in natural play. However, toward the end of your observation, you may ask the children to demonstrate any skill not seen in play.

Skill	Descriptive Phrases	
	3-year-old	5-year-old
Walking and variations, including whirling around		
Running		
Jumping		
Climbing		

(Continued)

Name_____

Skill	Descriptive Phrases	
	3-year-old	5-year-old
Throwing a ball		
Catching a ball		
Hopping		
Skipping		
Any tumbling skills		
Walking a balance beam (optional)		

Preschoolers Lack Complete Logical Thought

Activity A

Chapter 16

Name _____

Date _____ Period_____

Although preschoolers have advanced mentally, there are flaws in their thinking. Match the following stories with the types of obstacles to complete logical thought.

Obstacles

A. egocentrism
B. centering attention on one part
C. focusing on individual steps, stages, or events
D. not being able to mentally reverse action
E. associating actions without using logic or reasoning

Stories

_____ 1. Darnell is looking through the family album with his sister. His sister points to a picture of their father when he was five and says, "That's a really old picture of Daddy." Darnell shakes his head and insists that the picture is not of Daddy. When his sister asks why, Darnell says, "Daddy is a man—not a little boy!"

_____ 2. Denise is playing house under the card table and she invites the baby-sitter to join her in the house for lunch. When the baby-sitter says that the table is too small for him to fit, Denise takes him to the table. She crawls under and says, "The table's not too small. See—I fit!"

_____ 3. Jeff helped his parents plant a garden last month, and he knows that it needs rain to grow. Jeff is worried because it has not rained for a few weeks. As his father leaves for work that day, Jeff says, "Daddy, take your umbrella to work today." When his father asks why, Jeff replies, "So it will rain on the garden."

_____ 4. On their fourth birthday, Trina and Tracey each receive four silver dollars from their grandfather. One at a time, their grandfather has each girl count each coin as he hands it to her. Then he says, "There, you have four coins for your fourth birthday." Trina puts her money on the table in a stack, but Tracey spreads hers out in a line. When Tracey looks at Trina's coins, she asks, "Grandpa, how come you gave me more money than Trina?"

_____ 5. Mary is helping her mother make cutout cookies. Mary watches her mother take the ball of dough and divide it in half. Mary's mother gives half of the dough to Mary to roll out. Mary's mother rolls out the other half. After working with the dough a little while, Mary's mother has a large circle that is about one-fourth of an inch thick. Mary's circle is about an inch thick and much smaller. Mary says to her mother, "You gave me less dough because I'm littler, right?"

_____ 6. Tanya is going through an old train tunnel with her parents. When she sees the light at the end, she asks her parents what the light is. Her parents explain that the light is coming from the opening at the end of the tunnel. Tanya asks her parents, "How are we going to fit through that little hole?"

_____ 7. Andy's father had a large sack of popcorn that he was going to put into 20 jars to sell at a charity event. Andy watched his father pour all the popcorn from the sack into the jars. Andy asked his father what they would do if nobody wanted the popcorn. Andy's father asked, "What do you mean?" Andy said, "Well, there's no way we'll fit all that popcorn back in the sack!"

Using Symbols in Play

Activity B

Chapter 16

Name _____

Date _____ Period_____

Once children begin to use thought more, they make up symbols that they use in play. Symbols, which represent real objects, are most often portrayed in three main forms. First, preschool children use their bodies to represent something, such as jumping like a frog. Second, preschool children use their voices to represent something, such as using a low-pitched voice for Papa Bear. Third, preschool children use objects to represent other objects, such as using a leaf for a plate. Observe a group of preschool children in play and keep a list of the symbols you observe. Classify the symbols by form and record them in the space below.

Dates observed _____   Ages of children _____

Body Used as a Symbol

(Continued)

Name_____

Voice Used as a Symbol

Object Used as a Symbol

Fairy Tales and Children

Activity C

Chapter 16

Name _____

Date _____ Period_____

Preschool children give humanlike qualities to all living and nonliving objects. This thinking usually disappears in stages during the elementary school years. However, our culture sometimes makes it hard for children to tell which objects are human and which are nonhuman. List a fairy tale in our culture that may make these perceptions even stronger. Then, give examples of how humanlike qualities were given to living and nonliving objects in the story.

Example

1. Story _____*"The Three Little Pigs"*_____   *In this story, the pigs walk, talk, and dress like humans. They think like humans, take part in human activities (build houses, cook), and feel human emotions, such as fear of the wolf and joy when the wolf is conquered.*

2. Fairy tale _____

_____

_____

_____

_____

_____

_____

_____

_____

_____

_____

3. Describe how stories like these affect a child's thinking. _____

_____

_____

_____

_____

_____

_____

_____

_____

_____

A Dependable Adult

Activity A

Chapter 17

Name _____

Date _____ Period_____

Many parents and teachers ask children to be dependable. High school and college graduation speakers often cite the need for dependable as well as educated men and women. Husbands and wives who are happily married often refer to their marriage partners as dependable. Written references for jobs often require statements about a person's dependability. Dependability is a highly desirable characteristic that people need to develop. In the space below, list some examples of a dependable adult. Then answer the questions that follow.

A dependable adult is one who...

What are some advantages of being a dependable adult:

In the family setting?_____

_____

_____

_____

In the community setting?_____

_____

_____

_____

In the job setting? _____

_____

_____

_____

Friends Are Important

Activity B   Name _____

Chapter 17   Date _____ Period_____

With each year of growth and development, friends become more and more important to children. Friendships help physical, mental, and social-emotional development. Thus, the study of friendships is an important area of child development. Observe a group of preschoolers in play and give the information requested below.

1. Note several children who seemed well-liked by their peers. What traits do these children seem to possess?

_____

_____

_____

How do these traits of popular children compare with the traits of adults who are well-liked?_____

_____

_____

_____

Note some children who seemed to play alone for the most part. What traits do these children seem to possess?_____

_____

_____

How do these traits of unpopular children compare with the traits of adults who are not so popular?

_____

_____

_____

2. Ask two children individually (without other children close enough to hear), "What is a friend?"

Child A. Age _____ Gender _____ Definition of friendship _____

Child B. Age _____ Gender _____ Definition of friendship _____

How do these definitions compare with those suggested in your text?_____

_____

_____

3. Did a group or groups of two or three children form closed circles of friends who excluded others from play? _____ If so, describe what happened. _____

_____

_____

Why do you think other children were excluded? _____

_____

_____

_____

Learning from Play

Activity C

Chapter 17

Name _____

Date _____ Period _____

The social interaction children experience while playing with others helps them learn many concepts. Describe possible learnings children acquire when they play each of the following games with others.

Hide and Seek _____

_____

_____

_____

_____

_____

_____

_____

_____

_____

_____

_____

Trucks _____

_____

_____

_____

_____

_____

_____

_____

_____

_____

_____

_____

Dolls _____

_____

_____

_____

_____

_____

_____

_____

_____

_____

_____

Ball _____

_____

_____

_____

_____

_____

_____

_____

_____

_____

_____

Observation: Children at Play

Activity D

Chapter 17

Name _____

Date _____ Period_____

You can learn a great deal about children by watching them play. Observe children at play. As you observe, pay attention to the gender roles they use and to their conversation. Also, be aware of any emotions they display. Record your observations below.

1. First names and ages of children. _____

_____

_____

_____

2. What were the children doing?_____

_____

_____

_____

_____

3. Did you see "boy" activities? Describe them. _____

_____

_____

_____

_____

4. Did you see "girl" activities? Describe them. _____

_____

_____

_____

_____

5. Did you see any role reversal play? List examples. _____

_____

_____

_____

_____

6. What were the children talking about while they played?_____

_____

_____

_____

_____

_____

(Continued)

Name_____

7. Write out two dialogues you heard. _____

_____

_____

_____

_____

_____

_____

_____

_____

_____

_____

_____

_____

_____

8. Describe an observation of

   A. anger_____

   B. frustration_____

   C. jealousy _____

   D. fear _____

Date and time of observation._____

Providing for the Preschooler's Developmental Needs

18

Special Foods Are Fun

Activity A

Chapter 18

Name _____

Date _____ Period_____

Preschool children enjoy attractive-looking foods as much as adults do. Children are more apt to eat foods that are prepared especially for them. They also enjoy special plates, napkins, or centerpieces. Plan and serve a special meal or snack for a preschooler. You will need to examine recipe books and accompanying photos or drawings to get ideas. In the space below, provide the information requested.

1. What food(s) have you chosen? _____

_____

_____

_____

2. Record recipes below.

(Continued)

Name_____

3. Describe how you prepared the food, the dishes, napkins, or centerpiece especially for the child.

_____

_____

_____

_____

_____

_____

Make a drawing or glue a photo of the finished product below.

4. What are the child's reactions to the meal or snack? (Be specific by recording the child's comments as well as whether he or she ate the prepared food.) _____

_____

_____

_____

_____

5. If you were preparing this meal or snack again, what change(s) would you make? Give reasons for each change.

_____

_____

_____

_____

Evaluating Garments for Preschoolers

Activity B   Name _____

Chapter 18   Date _____ Period_____

Garments for preschoolers must be chosen with much care. Not only must a garment meet the same fabric and construction features as needed for toddlers, a garment for a preschooler must contain features that take into account growth patterns, safety needs, and self-dressing needs. Choose a garment and rate each feature on the scale. Write comments to explain your ratings. Share your ratings with other class members.

1. Describe the garment you have chosen. _____

_____

_____

_____

_____

_____

2. Rate each feature and make comments when necessary to justify your rating.

Features	Rating

Safety
    fire retardant
    no loose button or other parts
    belts and other features attached to garment
    wide pant legs or sleeves not gathered at cuff
    hoods that easily detach if caught
    easily visible (for outdoor night wear)
	1 2 3 4 5
	very not
	safe safe
	
	Comments

Comfort
    lightweight and absorbent fabrics
    stretch fabrics
    enough fullness for arms and knees to
      bend and stoop
    not binding
	1 2 3 4 5
	very not
	comfortable comfortable
	
	Comments

(Continued)

Name_____

Features	Rating
Allowance for growth stretch fabrics adjustable waistbands and shoulder straps two-piece outfits deep hems and large seams kimono or raglan sleeves	1 2 3 4 5 much none Comments
Quality of construction even stitches that are not too long flat seams reinforcement at points of strain matched checks and plaids: other attention to detail	1 2 3 4 5 high poor quality quality Comments
Care washable soil-release finish little or no ironing needed	1 2 3 4 5 easy difficult Comments
Self-dressing features large openings easy to recognize fronts and backs front opening elastic in waists and in wrists easy to work fasteners	1 2 3 4 5 many few Comments

Planned Observation Activities for Preschoolers

Activity C

Chapter 18

Name _____

Date _____ Period _____

From the observation activities you have read about and discussed, plan to try one or more of the activities with a preschool child. Encourage attention to detail and use of their senses of hearing, touching, smelling, and tasting. Answer the following, and report your experience to the class.

What observation activity will you do? _____

_____

_____

First name and age of child_____

_____

Outline the steps you used. _____

_____

_____

_____

_____

_____

How did the child react to the activity? _____

_____

_____

_____

_____

_____

What did the child say?_____

_____

_____

_____

_____

What did the child do? _____

_____

_____

_____

_____

(Continued)

Name_____

Was this a good activity? If not, how would you change it the next time? _____

_____

_____

_____

_____

_____

_____

_____

List another example of an observation activity. _____

_____

Date of completion _____

Problem-Solving Games—A Step Toward Logic

Activity D

Chapter 18

Name _____

Date _____ Period _____

For the most part, preschool children—like toddlers—learn during daily activities and as they play. Adults may add a few activities to enrich their learnings. Problem-solving activities are especially worthwhile for preschool children, because logical thinking concepts are not learned through the senses, but are mental concepts. Choose one activity from your text for each of the concepts to try with a child. Describe the activities below. Feel free to vary the activities to fit the situation. Try the chosen activities with a four- or five-year-old preschool child or children. It is recommended that you try no more than two activities in one sitting with the same preschool child. In fact, a preschool child may show interest in only one activity in one sitting.

Classification

Child's first name _____ Age _____ Gender _____

Brief Description of Game	Child's Interest and Learnings

Putting Objects in Order According to Size, Weight, or Volume

Child's first name _____ Age _____ Gender _____

Brief Description of Game	Child's Interest and Learnings

(Continued)

Name_____

Transformations

Child's first name _____ Age _____ Gender _____

Brief Description of Game	Child's Interest and Learnings

Reversals

Child's first name _____ Age _____ Gender _____

Brief Description of Game	Child's Interest and Learnings

Observation: Let's Pretend

Activity E

Chapter 18

Name _____

Date _____ Period_____

Preschoolers absorb themselves in pretend play. They can become monsters, kings or princesses, or whatever they choose. Observe a child (or children) at play. What symbols does he or she choose for make-believe play? You may suggest something for the child to act out. Perhaps the child will want to act out a story or idea through music or dance. Record your observations.

First name and ages of children _____

_____

_____

_____

_____

_____

What did the children act out, or who were they pretending to be?_____

_____

_____

_____

_____

_____

_____

Did they use any symbols to act out their idea? _____

_____

_____

_____

_____

_____

Did you interact by suggesting a theme or helping to carry out the make-believe story? Describe how. _____

_____

_____

_____

_____

_____

(Continued)

Name_____

Could the children tell pretend from reality? _____

_____

_____

_____

_____

_____

_____

_____

Is pretend play good for children? Why or why not?_____

_____

_____

_____

_____

_____

_____

Date of completion_____

Vocabulary Grows from Everyday Activities

Activity F

Chapter 18

Name _____

Date _____ Period_____

Talk between an adult and a child needs to be part of everyday activities. Adults may sometimes forget that talk that is part of day-to-day living activities can enrich a child's vocabulary. In the space below, list words that a preschool child may learn while observing or helping with these activities.

Meal Preparation, Meal Itself, and Cleanup

Bathing

Laundry

Cleaning House

(Continued)

Name_____

Gardening and Lawn Care

Car Cleaning

Shopping for Groceries

_____ (activity of your choice)

Helping with Tasks

Activity G

Chapter 18

Name _____

Date _____ Period_____

Preschool children want to help with tasks. Some tasks or parts of tasks are beyond the abilities of preschool children and may even be unsafe. Adults can select tasks or parts of tasks for preschoolers and explain how to do them. This helps the child learn new skills and the importance of helping others. For each task below, decide what the preschool child can do and how you can explain the task in order for the child to succeed and have fun.

Task	Part Child Can Do	Explanation of Task
Washing and drying dishes		
Vacuuming		
Washing car		
Putting away groceries		

(Continued)

Name_____

Task	Part Child Can Do	Explanation of Task
Helping with laundry		
Watering plants		
Dusting furniture		
Caring for a pet		
_____ (task of your choice)		

School-Age Children

Sports, Games, and Physical Qualities

Activity A

Chapter 19

Name _____

Date _____ Period _____

Sports and games require certain physical qualities, such as quick reaction time, for successful participation. Some sports and games center on one physical quality while other sports and games require two or more. In the space below, list sports and games that depend on the quality listed for successful participation. For sports or games that require two or more physical qualities, list the sport or game in each space. Explain why each quality was chosen. Then answer the question that follows. An example is shown to help you get started.

Reaction Time

Baseball—needed for hitting and catching

Precision

Speed

(Continued)

Name_____

Strength

Flexibility

Name a sport or game that requires three or more of the physical qualities. How are these qualities used for successful participation in the sport or game? _____

_____

_____

_____

_____

_____

Proper Diets Are Important in Middle Childhood

Activity B

Chapter 19

Name _____

Date _____ Period_____

Nutritious meals and snacks are important in middle childhood. Children at this age need food for present and future growth, for great energy demands, and for resisting infections. At this time, children are forming lifelong food habits, too. Using chart 19-7 of the text, plan a varied menu for a school-age child.

	Monday	Tuesday	Wednesday	Thursday	Friday
Breakfast					
Lunch					
Dinner					
Snack					

A School-Age Child's Bedroom

Activity C

Chapter 19

Name _____

Date _____ Period_____

School-age children need their own space for playing, studying, daydreaming, resting, and sleeping. Pretend you are planning a room for a school-age child. Choose and arrange the furniture. In the space below, respond to each of the steps.

1. Describe the child in terms of age, gender, and interests, such as hobbies. _____

   _____

   _____

   _____

   _____

2. Choose the furniture you would use in the room from the given furniture patterns. Trace the furniture patterns onto another sheet of paper. Cut out the traced patterns. Move them around on the bedroom floor plan below until you get a suitable arrangement, and then glue them in place.

Window

15′

Window

Door

Closet

20′

(Continued)

Name_____

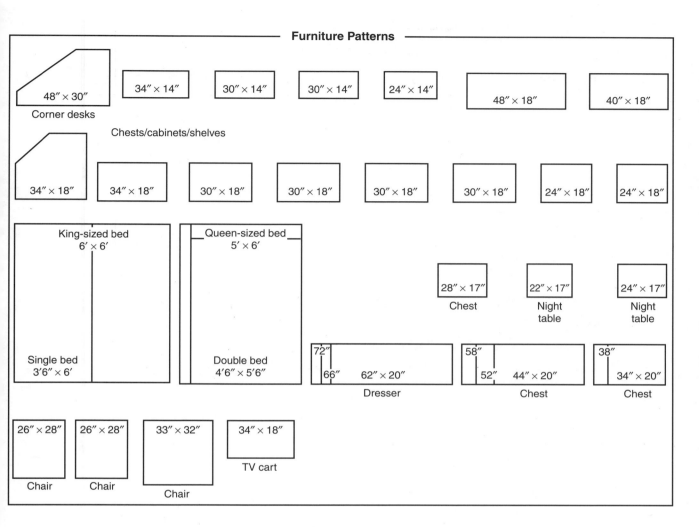

Furniture Patterns

3. In the space below, describe how you would decorate the room so it pleases the child. You may use pictures of furniture or accessories, color swatches, fabric samples, or other items. _____

_____

_____

_____

_____

_____

_____

_____

_____

_____

_____

_____

_____

(Continued)

Name_____

4. Evaluate your arrangement by answering the following questions:

Is your plan spatially pleasing with needed space around furniture? _____

(For instance, is there enough space to easily get in and out of a desk chair or room to make the bed?) _____ Explain why. _____

_____

_____

_____

_____

_____

Is enough space provided for the following:

resting? _____

dressing? _____

working on a hobby or hobbies? _____

displaying a collection? _____

storing clothes, shoes, play and hobby equipment, and books? _____

In what ways does your plan reflect the child's needs and interests? _____

_____

_____

_____

_____

_____

_____

_____

_____

_____

_____

_____

_____

_____

_____

_____

_____

_____

_____

"I Do and I Understand"

Activity D

Chapter 19

Name _____

Date _____ Period _____

An old Chinese proverb reads:

I hear and I forget.

I see and I remember.

I do and I understand.

Explain how the proverb applies to the mental development of school-age children. _____

_____

_____

_____

_____

_____

_____

_____

_____

_____

_____

_____

_____

_____

_____

_____

_____

_____

_____

_____

_____

_____

_____

_____

_____

_____

_____

Children's Humor: A Reflection of Mental and Language Development

Activity E

Chapter 19

Name _____

Date _____ Period _____

The development of the mind and language skills affects the humor that a child enjoys and understands. Thus, there is a developmental sequence to a child's view of humor. For example, young children enjoy action-type humor (such as clown actions). As children grow older, they begin to enjoy language humor (such as jokes). Find some examples of school-age children's humor and record examples in the space below.

Humor of Younger School-Age Children

1. Interview a six- or seven-year-old child.

Age _____ Grade level _____ Gender _____

What makes your friends laugh? _____

_____

_____

_____

Tell me something you have seen that was funny. _____

_____

_____

_____

Tell me a joke you like. _____

_____

_____

_____

2. Ask a primary-grade teacher or a librarian to show you humorous books enjoyed by primary grade children. Examine one of these books.

Name of author, title, and publisher _____

_____

Description of contents _____

_____

_____

_____

_____

_____

_____

_____

(Continued)

Name _____

Humor of Older School-Age Children

1. Interview a nine-, ten-, or eleven-year-old child.

   Age _____ Grade level _____ Gender _____

   What makes your friends laugh? _____

   _____

   _____

   _____

   Tell me something you have seen that was funny. _____

   _____

   _____

   _____

   Tell me a favorite joke. _____

   _____

   _____

   Tell me a favorite funny chant or song with words changed. _____

   _____

   _____

2. Ask an upper elementary grade teacher or a librarian to show you humorous books enjoyed by upper elementary grade children. Examine one of these books.

   Name of author, title, and publisher _____

   _____

   Description of contents _____

   _____

   _____

   _____

Differences in Humor

In general, what major differences do you see between the humor of school-age children in the primary grades and those in the upper elementary grades? _____

_____

_____

_____

_____

_____

_____

Industry Is Important in the School Years

Activity F

Chapter 19

Name _____

Date _____ Period_____

Middle childhood is the time for developing the attitudes needed for adult work. If these attitudes are encouraged, school-age children will develop a sense of industry. Interview a 10-, 11-, or 12-year-old child and record the child's responses in the space below. Then answer the question that follows.

Age _____ Grade level _____ Gender _____

What have you learned in your home, school, and organizations that will help you become a more skillful adult?

_____

_____

_____

_____

_____

_____

Although everyone likes to play at times, as people become older they have to work more and more. What can a boy or girl of your age learn from being expected to work in the home, the school, and in other places? (Try to get the child to answer in terms of work in general rather than focusing on skills acquired by working at a specific task.) _____

_____

_____

_____

_____

_____

_____

How does it make you feel when you contribute to work at home? _____

_____

_____

_____

_____

_____

_____

Peers Are Important

Activity G

Chapter 19

Name _____

Date _____ Period _____

Middle childhood is the age for exploring friendships with peers. Friendships are fun, but peers serve many other purposes as well. In the space below, give examples of how peers can fulfill each of the purposes listed.

1. Close friendships are formed. _____

_____

_____

_____

_____

2. Peers provide the chance to join formal groups. _____

_____

_____

_____

_____

3. Peers help children depend less on adults. _____

_____

_____

_____

_____

4. Peers provide emotional support. _____

_____

_____

_____

_____

5. Peers share information. _____

_____

_____

_____

_____

6. Peers affect self-concept. _____

_____

_____

_____

_____

School-Age Children Want to Be Accepted

Activity H

Chapter 19

Name _____

Date _____ Period_____

All people want to be accepted as they are. School-age children are developing their first close friendships with adults outside family and with peers. They especially need to be accepted without too many strings attached. In the space below, write an essay that includes these points: (a) What does it mean to be accepted as we are? (b) Why is acceptance without too may strings attached needed to develop good relationships with others?

_____

_____

_____

_____

_____

_____

_____

_____

_____

_____

_____

_____

_____

_____

_____

_____

_____

_____

_____

_____

_____

_____

_____

_____

_____

_____

_____

Helping Children Deal with Rejection

Activity I   Name _____

Chapter 19   Date _____ Period_____

Friends and other peers are important to school-age children. Because of this, fear of rejection is very real during middle childhood. Adults can help when children experience general rejection or when they lose their close friends. In the following situations, explain how you would respond to help the child. (Include actions you would take as well as what you would say.)

1. Sue comes home from school and doesn't say a word. When you ask her what's wrong, she says that all the kids at school pick on her. "When the teacher asks me to read out loud, I can't say any of the words right," says Sue. "I know what the words are, but I just get scared. Then all the kids laugh and say I'm stupid."

   Your response _____

   _____

   _____

   _____

   _____

2. You are with Manuel when a group of his classmates walk by. Manuel says they are going to the park. When you ask why Manuel isn't going, he says, "They didn't ask me. They're going to play softball, and they know I strike out every time."

   Your response _____

   _____

   _____

   _____

   _____

3. You are helping to plan a picnic for a third grade class. Sandra approaches you and says she doesn't want to go. When you ask why, she says, "They always have races and I'm always way behind. Everyone laughs at me."

   Your response _____

   _____

   _____

   _____

   _____

4. Mark is sitting at home on a Saturday. When you ask why he is not playing with the other children across the street, he says, "Paul doesn't want to be my best friend any more because he has a new best friend. If I can't play with Paul, I might as well stay home."

   Your response _____

   _____

   _____

   _____

   _____

Teaching Through Play

20

Learning Through Play

Activity A

Chapter 20

Name _____

Date _____ Period_____

The founder of kindergarten, Friedrich Froebel, called play the highest level of child development. Play aids motor skills, emotional well-being, and even learning. Play activities result in learnings about attributes of objects, logical knowledge concepts, use of symbols, and vocabulary. In the space below, give examples of what children may learn from play.

Hide and Seek	
Attributes of Objects	Logical Knowledge Concepts
Use of Symbols	Vocabulary

Block Building	
Attributes of Objects	Logical Knowledge Concepts
Use of Symbols	Vocabulary

(Continued)

Name_____

Playing House

Attributes of Objects	Logical Knowledge Concepts
Use of Symbols	Vocabulary

Working Jigsaw Puzzles

Attributes of Objects	Logical Knowledge Concepts
Use of Symbols	Vocabulary

Playing Board Games

Attributes of Objects	Logical Knowledge Concepts
Use of Symbols	Vocabulary

Development Through the Visual Arts

Activity B   Name _____

Chapter 20   Date _____ Period_____

Most children enjoy creating in the visual arts. Besides the pleasure, creating in the visual arts promotes development in many areas. Observe a preschool or school-age child creating in the visual arts. In the space below, record your observations.

Age of child _____ Gender _____

Photograph or description of art work.

Describe the fine-motor skills creating the artwork aided (handling paintbrush, cutting with scissors). _____

_____

_____

What sensory learnings (color, texture, size, shape) did it promote?_____

_____

_____

What learnings did children express in content (some trees have leaves, grass is green)? _____

_____

_____

What feelings did children express (sadness shown in content of art product, pride in art product itself)?

_____

_____

Learning Science Through Cooking

Activity C

Chapter 20

Name _____

Date _____ Period_____

Children can learn many science concepts through cooking. Adults should point out concepts as children try their hands at cooking. Plan and conduct a cooking lesson with a nine- to twelve-year-old child. In the space below, write or mount the chosen recipe for the cooking lesson. List the supplies, including ingredients and utensils, that you will need for the lesson. Then list some concepts you might explain as important learnings to the child as you cook. After the lesson, evaluate what the child actually learned.

Recipe _____

Supplies Needed

_____

_____

_____

_____

_____

_____

_____

_____

(Continued)

Name_____

1. **Importance of being clean and taking safety measures**

   Concepts you plan to explain or demonstrate _____

   _____

   _____

   Evaluation of child's learning_____

   _____

   _____

2. **Need to follow directions in order and to complete a task**

   Concepts you plan to explain or demonstrate _____

   _____

   _____

   Evaluation of child's learnings _____

   _____

   _____

3. **Use of all senses**

   Concepts you plan to explain or demonstrate _____

   _____

   _____

   Evaluation of child's learnings _____

   _____

   _____

4. **Need to carefully count and measure**

   Concepts you plan to explain or demonstrate _____

   _____

   _____

   Evaluation of child's learnings _____

   _____

   _____

5. **Understanding basic chemical changes**

   Concepts you plan to explain or demonstrate _____

   _____

   _____

   Evaluation of child's learnings _____

   _____

   _____

(Continued)

Name_____

6. **Use of motor skills**

Concepts you plan to explain or demonstrate _____

_____

_____

Evaluation of child's learnings _____

_____

_____

7. **Knowledge of nutrition**

Concepts you plan to explain or demonstrate _____

_____

_____

Evaluation of child's learnings _____

_____

_____

8. **Sources of foods and ways foods are prepared and served**

Concepts you plan to explain or demonstrate _____

_____

_____

Evaluation of child's learnings _____

_____

_____

9. **Names of foods and food groups**

Concepts you plan to explain or demonstrate _____

_____

_____

Evaluation of child's learnings _____

_____

_____

10. **Understanding of cooking equipment and cooking processes**

Concepts you plan to explain or demonstrate _____

_____

_____

Evaluation of child's learnings _____

_____

_____

Protecting Children's Health and Safety

Adults Model Health Practices

Activity A

Chapter 21

Name _____

Date _____ Period_____

Children learn a lot by watching adults. Children often imitate what they see adults do. Much of what children imitate becomes part of their own habits, because young children consider adult actions to be important. This modeling includes health practices. In the space below, list examples of good health practices adults can model for children in terms of nutrition, rest, cleanliness, and exercise.

Nutrition _____

_____

_____

_____

_____

Rest _____

_____

_____

_____

_____

Cleanliness _____

_____

_____

_____

_____

Exercise _____

_____

_____

_____

_____

_____

Supervision Decreases Accidents

Activity B

Chapter 21

Name _____

Date _____ Period_____

Accidents often happen when there is not enough adult supervision. Certainly it is difficult for even the most well-meaning adults to be aware of everything children do. However, careful planning can make for better supervision. In the space below, suggest some ways adults may increase supervision during difficult times.

Suggestions for increasing supervision when . . .

. . . older children are supervising younger children _____

_____

_____

_____

_____

_____

_____

_____

_____

_____

_____

_____

. . . adults are busy with chores, such as supper preparation _____

_____

_____

_____

_____

_____

_____

_____

_____

_____

_____

_____

. . . adults are not feeling well or are very ill _____

_____

_____

_____

_____

_____

_____

_____

_____

_____

_____

_____

. . . adults need time to think about their own concerns _____

_____

_____

_____

_____

_____

_____

_____

_____

_____

_____

_____

Childproofing Is Essential

Activity C

Chapter 21

Name _____

Date _____ Period_____

Adults must look around their homes and note dangerous objects or situations in children's worlds. Pretend you are preparing to childproof a room in a home. As you look around a room of your choice, evaluate all of the areas listed below that apply to the room. Then list any childproofing measures you would need to take in that area.

Area	Comments on Safety	Childproofing Measures Needed
Areas with cords		
Areas with curtains		
Doors		
Electrical outlets		
Fans		

(Continued)

Name_____

Area	Comments on Safety	Childproofing Measures Needed
Fireplaces, open heaters, registers, and floor furnaces		
Furniture		
Rugs, area and throw		
Stairs		
Tubs		
Wastebaskets and garbage cans		
Windows		

Toys Should Not Hurt

Activity D   Name _____

Chapter 21   Date _____ Period_____

Toys can cause accidents for several reasons. Toys may not be properly made. Children may be too young or immature for the toys. Children may play with toys in unsafe ways. Toys may become unsafe after they break or wear. Adults need to consider toy safety. Choose a toy to evaluate. As you examine the toy, provide the information requested below.

Name of toy_____

Manufacturer or distributor _____

Does the label suggest suitable ages or cautions for use? _____

_____

Does the toy seem durable? _____

Explain why or why not._____

_____

_____

_____

Does the toy meet the safety measures listed in chart 21-13 of the text? _____

_____

Explain your answer giving safe and/or unsafe features of the toy._____

_____

_____

_____

_____

_____

_____

_____

What type of adult supervision is required for use of the toy? _____

_____

_____

_____

_____

If the toy is designed for older children, could it be harmful to an infant, toddler, or young child?_____

_____

_____

(Continued)

Name_____

If yes, in what way or ways? _____

_____

_____

_____

_____

Suggest how the adult could protect the too young or immature child from harm because of the toy._____

_____

_____

_____

_____

How much space is needed for use of the toy? _____

_____

What, if any, special requirements are there for use of the toy (such as resilient flooring, electrical outlet)? ____

_____

_____

_____

_____

_____

How much space is needed for storage of the toy? _____

_____

What, if any, special requirements are there for storage of the toy? _____

_____

Taking into account all of the above considerations, would you purchase the toy from a *safety standpoint?* ____

_____

What, if any, restrictions would you place on the toy's suitability from a *safety standpoint?* _____

_____

_____

_____

_____

_____

_____

_____

_____

_____

_____

Making Computers Child-Friendly

Activity E

Chapter 21

Name _____

Date _____ Period_____

Interview the parent of a child who uses a computer in the home. Ask the parent the following questions and record his or her responses below.

1. How old is your child, and how long has he or she been using the computer? _____
_____

2. For what purposes does your child use the computer (learning or homework, family activities, or fun)?
_____

3. Do you and your child talk about computer activities? _____
   If so, what do you share? _____
   _____
   _____

4. In what ways did you design or rearrange the computer area for your child's physical comfort and safety?
   _____
   _____

5. What guidelines do you follow in selecting (or aiding in the selection) of software? _____
   _____
   _____

6. How do you monitor computer use? (If filter is mentioned, ask about type of filter.) _____
   _____
   _____

7. What rules or guidelines have you set for your children's computer use? _____
   _____
   _____
   _____
   _____

8. What are your main concerns about children using computers? _____
   _____
   _____
   _____
   _____

Ill Children Need Quiet Activities

Activity F

Chapter 21

Name _____

Date _____ Period_____

Time passes slowly for an ill child. Time goes faster, and recovery may even be helped, when the child has a variety of quiet activities. In the space below, write two special quiet activities for an ill toddler, an ill preschool child, and an ill school-age child.

Toddler

Activity 1_____

_____

_____

_____

Activity 2_____

_____

_____

_____

Preschool Child

Activity 1_____

_____

_____

_____

Activity 2_____

_____

_____

_____

School-Age Child

Activity 1_____

_____

_____

_____

Activity 2_____

_____

_____

_____

Child Care and Education in Group Settings

The Shapes and Sizes of Children's Programs

Activity A

Chapter 22

Name _____

Date _____ Period_____

Programs for young children come in all shapes and sizes. The name of a program does not always tell what it is. Various programs for young children came from different roots. They admit different types of children, have different sponsorships and ownerships, and serve different purposes. As you read about each type of program in the text, complete the information in the space below.

In-Home Child Care

Children served _____

Sponsorship _____

Major purposes of program _____

_____

_____

Family Child Care

Children served _____

Sponsorship _____

Major purposes of program _____

_____

_____

Center-Based Child Care

Children served _____

Sponsorship _____

Major purposes of program _____

_____

_____

(Continued)

Name_____

Kindergartens

Children served _____

Sponsorship _____

Major purposes of program _____

_____

_____

Nursery Schools

Children served _____

Sponsorship _____

Major purposes of program _____

_____

_____

Montessori Schools

Children served _____

Sponsorship _____

Major purposes of program _____

_____

_____

Head Start

Children served _____

Sponsorship _____

Major purposes of program _____

_____

_____

Local Child Care and Education Facilities

Activity B

Chapter 22

Name _____

Date _____ Period_____

Pretend you are a parent who has just moved to your community. You are seeking a group program for your infant starting now and lasting for the next several years. Locate the local group (not in-home or family) child care and education services in your community (or in a nearby community if group child care is not available locally). If you live in a large city, restrict your search to one section of the city. Record your findings in the space below.

Name, Address, and Phone Number	Children Admitted	Notes on Program, Special Services, and Costs	Hours	Licensed (yes or no)
Not-for-Profit Centers				

(Continued)

Name_____

	For-Profit Centers			
Name, Address, and Phone Number	Children Admitted	Notes on Program, Special Services, and Costs	Hours	Licensed (yes or no)

Family Communication and Participation Opportunities

Activity C

Chapter 22

Name _____

Date _____ Period_____

Child care and education programs have had a rich tradition of parent involvement. Today's quality programs continue in this tradition. After studying Figure 22-15, visit one or two local group programs and get specifics on how they communicate with and involve families. Record your findings in the space below.

Name of program _____

Location _____

Description of communication or involvement (be specific) _____

_____

_____

_____

_____

_____

_____

_____

_____

_____

Name of program _____

Location _____

Description of communication or involvement (be specific) _____

_____

_____

_____

_____

_____

_____

_____

_____

_____

Good Programs Help Children Grow

Activity D

Chapter 22

Name _____

Date _____ Period _____

Good programs for young children use both routine activities (such as washing hands, eating, or cleaning up) and specially planned activities to help children grow. Visit a program for young children, then provide the information requested in the space below. Interview the director (or main teacher) and observe to obtain the needed information.

Name of program _____

Ages of children served_____

Hours of operation _____

Group observed _____

_____

List some of the main goals of the program. _____

_____

_____

_____

_____

_____

_____

Give some examples of some of the learnings presented through the day-to-day routines. _____

_____

_____

_____

_____

_____

_____

Describe some of the children's activities and materials used in as many of these areas as you can.

A. Language learnings _____

_____

_____

_____

_____

B. Mathematics learnings_____

_____

_____

_____

_____

(Continued)

Name_____

C. Social learnings _____

_____

_____

_____

_____

D. Science learnings_____

_____

_____

_____

_____

E. Creative fun _____

_____

_____

_____

_____

F. Motor skills _____

_____

_____

_____

_____

Give some examples of how the adults helped the children learn._____

_____

_____

_____

_____

_____

_____

_____

_____

_____

_____

_____

_____

_____

_____

_____

_____

_____

Finding a Quality Group Program

Activity E

Chapter 22

Name _____

Date _____ Period_____

Adults should check group programs carefully before choosing a program for a child. Finding a quality program can be difficult because adults must look beyond the appearance of the program's housing and equipment. In the following story, look for problems in the child care program. Then list the problems with ways of correcting them in the space that follows.

    Mrs. Rand was interested in placing her daughter, Sarah, in the Shady Tree child care program. She made an appointment to visit and meet with the owner, Ms. Mendez. When Mrs. Rand arrived at the center, Ms. Mendez was on the phone with the father of an enrolled child.

    "I'm sorry, Mr. O'Keefe, but we only allow parents to visit on Thursdays," Ms. Mendez was saying. "Having parents visit any time often interrupts our routines ... I'm glad you understand ... Don't worry, we're taking good care of Jeffrey ... Good-bye."

    Ms. Mendez quickly greeted Mrs. Rand in a cheery manner and began a tour of the center.

    "Because Sandy is three, she would be in our toddler group," said Ms. Mendez. She took Mrs. Rand into a room with cheery decorations. About 20 children were playing in the room. A 16-year-old girl was watching them.

    "This is Reena," said Ms. Mendez. "She helps out at the center after school. Another lady helps in the morning. Our full-time supervisor is Mr. Green. He has a bachelor's degree in child development. I would introduce you to him, but he's busy preparing a special afternoon snack for the children. Mr. Green is great with the children. Why, he makes sure all of the children can read several words before they leave the toddler program."

    Ms. Mendez finished the tour and thanked Mrs. Rand for her visit. The next day, Mrs. Rand called to say that she would not be enrolling Sarah in the Shady Tree program.

List problems you notice with the program and possible ways to correct them._____

_____

_____

_____

_____

_____

_____

_____

_____

_____

_____

_____

_____

_____

_____

_____

A More In-Depth View

Activity A

Chapter 23

Name _____

Date _____ Period _____

Experts have given society a deeper understanding of all forms of special needs. In the space below, provide information about one specific area of giftedness and about one specific type of disability or impairment. You may find more information from library sources, special education teachers, and people active in community agencies that work on behalf of children with special needs.

One Type Giftedness

Area of giftedness (such as mental, artistic, or other) _____

Statistics on children _____

_____

_____

Traits _____

_____

_____

_____

_____

_____

Method of identification (such as tests, auditions) _____

_____

_____

_____

Programs, agencies, associations, and other resources for meeting needs _____

_____

_____

_____

_____

_____

_____

_____

_____

(Continued)

Name_____

One Type of Disability or Impairment

Area of disability or impairment_____

Statistics on children _____

_____

_____

Traits _____

_____

_____

_____

_____

Method of identification (such as tests) _____

_____

_____

_____

Programs, agencies, associations, and other resources for meeting needs_____

_____

_____

_____

_____

_____

_____

_____

_____

_____

_____

A Special Classroom

Activity B   Name _____

Chapter 23   Date _____ Period _____

Classrooms for children with special needs are common today. Because children with special needs are more like other children than different, all classrooms share many things in common. However, classrooms must be adapted to meet these children's special needs. Observe in a classroom for children with special needs and speak with the teacher. In the space below, provide the information requested.

Type of special needs represented in the classroom _____

Admission requirements (such as age of child, type of special need) _____

_____

_____

Adaptation of facility (such as ramps) _____

_____

_____

_____

Types of instructional materials used _____

_____

_____

_____

_____

Method of teaching _____

_____

_____

_____

Special services provided (such as health, transportation) _____

_____

_____

_____

Number of children in one classroom_____

_____

_____

Number of teachers and other adults _____

_____

_____

How does this classroom compare with a typical classroom? _____

_____

_____

_____

Community Resources

Activity C

Chapter 23

Name _____

Date _____ Period_____

Many communities have resources designed to help children with special needs, their parents, and other adults who care for them. Locate some of these sources in your community or a nearby community. Give information on the services in the space provided below.

Name, address, and telephone of resource _____
_____

Sponsorship (such as government agency, private group) _____

Type of children served (include special need, age range, and other qualifications)_____
_____

Services provided _____
_____
_____

Name, address, and telephone of resource _____
_____

Sponsorship (such as government agency, private group) _____

Type of children served (include special need, age range, and other qualifications)_____
_____

Services provided _____
_____
_____

Name, address, and telephone of resource _____
_____

Sponsorship (such as government agency, private group) _____

Type of children served (include special need, age range, and other qualifications)_____
_____

Services provided _____
_____
_____

Name, address, and telephone of resource _____
_____

Sponsorship (such as government agency, private group) _____

Type of children served (include special need, age range, and other qualifications)_____
_____

Services provided _____
_____
_____

The Roles of Siblings

Activity A

Chapter 24

Name _____

Date _____ Period _____

Most children in the United States grow up with at least one sibling. Siblings spend so much time together that they cannot help but influence each other's lives. Siblings serve as playmates, teachers and learners, protectors, and rivals. For each of the roles listed below, give specific examples of how siblings have filled these roles. You may use examples from your own experience or interview someone else who has siblings.

Playmates

Teachers and Learners

Protectors

Rivals

Working Parents Must Be Good Managers

Activity B

Chapter 24

Name _____

Date _____ Period _____

Trying to handle the demands of a home and a job is difficult at times. Working parents who are good managers seem to be successful in meeting their many demands. Interview a working parent about how he or she balances family and work demands. In the space below, record the information requested. Share your interview responses with other class members.

Other members of the family (husband, wife, number and ages of children) _____

Father's or mother's career _____

_____

There are many demands you must fulfill. Please describe some ways you manage each of the following demands.

Time for your family _____

_____

_____

_____

_____

Time for home care tasks and errands _____

_____

_____

_____

_____

Time for job tasks beyond regular working hours _____

_____

_____

_____

_____

Time for yourself _____

_____

_____

_____

_____

_____

(Continued)

Name_____

Do you have to establish priorities? Explain. _____

_____

_____

_____

_____

Do you let some tasks go completely undone? Explain. _____

_____

_____

_____

_____

How do you let your family know how to help you?_____

_____

_____

_____

_____

Under what circumstances do you find it the hardest to fulfill your many demands?_____

_____

_____

_____

_____

How do you cope with feelings of not always being able to successfully meet your many demands?_____

_____

_____

_____

_____

What is positive about being a working parent?_____

_____

_____

_____

_____

What is negative about being a working parent? _____

_____

_____

_____

Planning Ahead for Self-Care

Activity C

Chapter 24

Name _____

Date _____ Period_____

Pretend you are an adult responsible for the care of a school-age child. This child will be alone after school. In the space below, give the background information requested. Then list five concerns you might have for the well-being of this child. Follow with possible solutions for each concern. Share your ideas with your classmates.

Background information (age of child, home and community setting) _____

_____

_____

_____

_____

Concern _____

Solution _____

_____

_____

_____

Concern _____

Solution _____

_____

_____

_____

Concern _____

Solution _____

_____

_____

_____

Concern _____

Solution _____

_____

_____

_____

Concern _____

Solution _____

_____

_____

_____

Grief and Other Reactions to Death

Activity D

Chapter 24

Name _____

Date _____ Period_____

Death and grief are difficult for a child to understand. Young children find it hard to understand why death cannot be reversed. They grieve over the loss of a loved person or pet. Adults should carefully plan their responses to children concerning death and grief even before a death occurs. Confusion and guilt may arise in a child when an adult gives inappropriate reactions. For each of the situations below, record why the adult response is not appropriate and write a more appropriate reaction.

Situation	Reason Reaction Is Inappropriate	More Appropriate Reaction
Samantha, a three-year-old, sat through a rather long funeral for her grandmother. At the cemetery, she freed herself from her mother and began to play in the fallen leaves. Her mother walked over to her, brought her back, and said, "If you really loved your grandmother, you would not be playing."		
When four-year-old Shane asked about his grandfather who had died, Shane's father said, "Grandpa is on a long trip."		
Tom, who was three years old, lost his father in a car accident. His grieving mother left Tom with strangers for a couple of days while she took care of funeral arrangements and legal matters.		

(Continued)

Name_____

Situation	Reason Reaction Is Inappropriate	More Appropriate Reaction
Tanisha asked, "Where did Becky go?" (Becky, who was Tanisha's age, died after a lengthy illness.) Tanisha was then given a very detailed account of the family's religious beliefs.		
John's father told his five-year-old son to quit crying about Dusty, because "she was only a dog."		
Richard, a three-year-old child, and Michael, his five-year-old brother, were acting out their aunt's funeral. Their parents stopped their pretend play by saying, "You should never pretend to die."		
Juan was concerned following his grandfather's death. He had been especially close to his grandfather. In an effort to comfort her four-year-old son, Juan's mother said, "Don't worry, I'll never die and leave you!"		

Teen Parenting: A Major Risk

Activity E   Name _____

Chapter 24   Date _____ Period_____

Parenting can be a rewarding task under the right conditions and at the right time. Listed below are five of the reasons for not choosing parenthood that were given in Chapter 3. As you read the text section "Teens as Parents," explain how each of these reasons might apply to a teen couple and why having a baby despite this reason would be a major risk. Then give other reasons you think teen parenting might be a major risk.

"We're not ready for a child." _____

_____

_____

_____

"A baby costs a lot." _____

_____

_____

_____

"A child will tie us down." _____

_____

_____

_____

"A child will interfere with our career plans." _____

_____

_____

_____

"Our child could be sick or disabled." _____

_____

_____

_____

"Our marriage could fail, and I don't want to be a single parent." _____

_____

_____

Other reasons: _____

_____

_____

_____

Traits of Child Abusers

Activity F

Chapter 24

Name _____

Date _____ Period _____

Throughout history, child abuse has been a serious problem. Recently, research has not only focused on how to help abused children, but also on how to help adults before they become abusers. Child abusers have been found to have certain traits. Of course, not all adults who have these traits are child abusers. For adults with each of the following traits, explain why the trait may lead to child abuse.

Adults who believe that physical force should be used to punish children _____

_____

_____

_____

Adults who were abused as children_____

_____

_____

_____

Adults who lack self-esteem _____

_____

_____

_____

Adults who feel alone because they are away from relatives or do not have close friends _____

_____

_____

_____

Adults who are under very high amounts of stress_____

_____

_____

_____

Adults who set goals too high for their children _____

_____

_____

_____

Making Career Decisions

My Interests, Aptitudes, and Abilities

Activity A

Chapter 25

Name _____

Date _____ Period_____

At this stage in your life, you should begin to think about a career choice. Your answers to the following questions will help you focus on your interests (1-6), aptitudes (7-12), and future abilities (13-15). Think carefully before writing answers in the spaces provided. Briefly explain each answer.

1. Why is knowing about children's development important to you?
   - Is it because children's development is the foundation for life?
   - Is it because children affect family relations and resources?
   - Is it because children need special products and services?

2. What do you find most interesting about children?
   - Is it their thinking, talk, curiosity, and emotions?
   - Is it the challenge they present to parents and other adults?
   - Is it the complexity of their development?
   - Is it their needs for special products and services?

3. Would you prefer contact with children or adults?

4. Would you prefer to be seen as a
   - sensitive and caring person?
   - knowledgeable person?
   - creative person?

5. Would you prefer to
   - work on your own project?
   - be part of a team effort?
   - lead a team?

(Continued)

6. Are you interested primarily in working
   - in a direct service career?
   - in a consultant career?
   - in other fields that may involve children, such as a dietitian?

7. Are you talented in
   - nurturing children?
   - explaining ideas to adults?
   - creating new things or ideas?

8. What other talents do you have?

9. Can you cope with constant change and a hectic pace?

10. Can you anticipate needs of others?

11. Can you communicate well?

12. Do you get along well with others?

13. Would you prefer to
    - seek a college degree?
    - enter a career upon high school graduation?

14. What specific experiences with children have you had?

15. What abilities or skills have you developed or learned that will help you work in a child-related career?

16. What abilities or skills do you plan to develop or learn that will help you work in a child-related career?

Getting Involved

Activity B

Chapter 25

Name _____

Date _____ Period_____

Many people in the local community have careers in child-related fields. The first step in getting involved is getting to know those people. Often, those established in careers help others get started by offering advice and sometimes chances for experience (with and without pay). In the space below, complete the following information about people in your area with child-related careers.

1. Name of person_____

   Address and telephone number _____

   _____

   Preferred hours for contact_____

   Description of person's career _____

   _____

   _____

   _____

2. Name of person_____

   Address and telephone number _____

   _____

   Preferred hours for contact _____

   Description of person's career _____

   _____

   _____

   _____

3. Name of person_____

   Address and telephone number _____

   _____

   Preferred hours for contact_____

   Description of person's career _____

   _____

   _____

   _____

4. Name of person_____

   Address and telephone number _____

   _____

   Preferred hours for contact_____

   Description of person's career _____

   _____

   _____

Presenting Yourself

Activity C

Chapter 25

Name _____

Date _____ Period_____

Resumes sum up your experiences and present them in a complete format that is easy to understand. You can use a resume to seek admission to college or other training programs, to find a job, and to earn a scholarship. You can begin preparing your resume now. A real resume should be neatly typed or professionally printed on quality paper. They must be accurate and positive. Resumes also must be reviewed from time to time and brought up to date. In the space below, provide information to use on your resume.

Name _____

Address _____

Telephone number(s)_____

Membership in organizations and offices held _____

_____

_____

Honors received_____

_____

_____

Work experiences _____

_____

_____

_____

_____

_____

Special skills and interests _____

_____

_____

_____

_____

_____

*References (names and addresses of two or three individuals) _____

_____

_____

_____

_____

_____

_____

*Be sure to ask individuals whether they will serve as references before listing their names.